The Book of Clouds

The Book of Clouds

by
Oludamini Ogunnaike

FONS VITAE

First published in 2023 by
Fons Vitae
49 Mockingbird Valley Drive
Louisville, KY 40207
http://www.fonsvitae.com
Email: fonsvitaeky@aol.com

Library of Congress Control Number: 2023951421

ISBN 978-1941610-961

Printed in South Korea

Contents

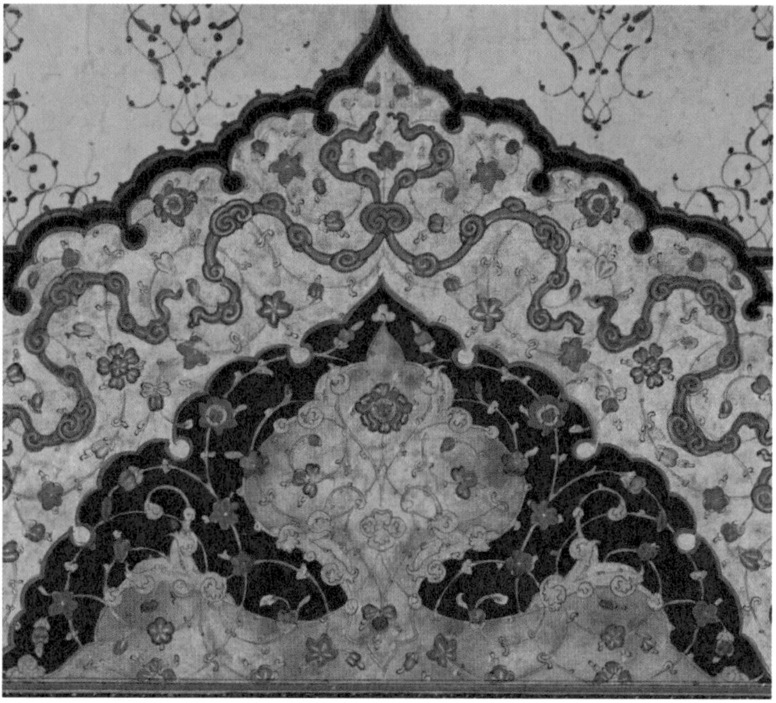

بسم الله الرحمن الرحيم
الحمد للّه ربّ العالمين
والصلاة والسّلام على أشرف المرسلين
و أحبّ المحبّين و صبّ العاشقين
و سيّد الكونين و قرّة العينين
صاحب قاب قوسين
وأدنى
ذي الآيات الكبرى
و جوامع الكلم
و الحمد الأتمّ
ممدّ الهمم
ومداد النور و قلمه
وعلى آله الكرام
إرثه الكريم
حقّ قدره ومقداره العظيم

In the shifting of the winds and the clouds subdued between the heaven and the earth are surely signs for a people who understand

—Qur'an, The Cow, 164

And you see the mountains, supposing them solid, while they are passing away as passing clouds...

—Qur'an, *The Ant*, 88

He it is Who sends the winds as tidings heralding His mercy, so that when they bear heavy clouds, We drive them to a dead land, and then send down water upon it and thereby bring forth every kind of fruit. Thus We bring forth the dead, that haply you may remember

—Qur'an, *The Heights*, 57

"Where was God before He created creation?" "He was in a cloud above which was no air, and below which there was no air."

—Hadith

When I am dead, open my grave and see
The cloud of smoke that rises round thy feet;
In my dead heart the fire still burns for thee;
Yea, the smoke rises from my winding sheet!

—Hafez, translated by Getrude Bell

بسم الله الرحمن الرحيم

Foreword

This collection of poems by Oludamini Ogunnaike represents a bold pathway for the appreciation of Sufi literary aesthetics in the English language. These original poems draw inspiration from a number of cultures and literary traditions, but most prominent to me are the love lyrics known as *ghazal*s.

Terse and often focused on one particular love-based theme, *ghazal*s can traditionally be found in Arabic, Persian, Urdu, and Turkish literature—among other languages. Like Ogunnaike's poems, *ghazal*s represent a fusion of various cultural and artistic values that permeated Islamicate societies. In the case of many of the poems here, in terms of style, you will see *ghazal*-like structures throughout. These include the *radīf*, which is a word or phrase that appears at the end of each verse along with the rhyming word, the *takhalluṣ* or pen name (in this case, Sulayman or Solomon) used to "sign off" ghazals at their end, as well as certain important stock characters, such as the *rind,* which Ogunnaike ingeniously translates as the "gangster rascal lover of God." However, other stock figures and images are transformed: the "Magian Pir" of the Persian poetic tradition—representing the sincere Sufi master, reviled by religious authorities precisely for his or her sincerity—appears here as a "Babalawo," a priest of traditional Yoruba religion. Poetic devices from the ghazal tradition, such as *jinās* (pun/paronomasia) also adorn Ogunnaike's poetry. For example, in the beginning of this ghazal:

How could you leave me all alone?
    Even Adam didn't fall alone

"Even Adam" sounds like "Eve and Adam." While the beginning of another ghazal illustrates a clever use of the feature of *ṭibāq* (antithesis), where "truth" is contrasted with "lying":

Truth is, for me, hell, with you'd be heaven
    Lying in your arms, this world beats heaven

The poems in this collection also represent an adaptation of the quantitative meters of Arabic and Persian into a hybrid qualitative/syllabic-metered English; for example, the ghazal that begins:

> When I could, I knew not; when I knew, I could not
> though sun's light sees all sights, its own view, eyes could not

is written in an anapest/Mutadarik meter (*faʿilun faʿilun faʿilun faʿilun*), and the ghazal that begins:

> This heart's a coal that pulses with each sweet gust of your breath
> hidden beneath this body of ash dancing on your breath

is written in something like the Basīṭ meter (*Mustafʿilun Fāʿilun Mustafʿilun Fāʿilun*), so it can be recited in the same melodies used for poems like al-Buṣīrī's *Burda*, also written in that meter. Ogunnaike's poetry is also threaded with double-entendres and subtle allusions to Arabic and other languages in lines such as these:

> And lo, but for you, my life would be lack
> and so, without you, my love's just abstract

which reference the tradition about the Prophet popular amongst Sufis, "If not for you, We would not have created the spheres," which in Arabic is "*Low lak ma khalaqna'l-aflak.*" Similarly, the opening line of this ghazal:

> What's all this murmuring?
> these voices that cried out?
> The hubbub of lovers'
> bubbles turned inside-out

plays on the common Arabic/Persian/Urdu ghazal figure of *ḥabāb* ("bubbles") and *aḥbāb* ("lovers"), both derived from the same root as *ḥubb* ("love"). While the short poem that begins "All of my sin is worship, and all of my worship's sin," plays on the fact that (as I've been informed) in Yoruba, "sìn" means "to worship."

While Persian and Arabic *ghazal*s might seem distant to English speakers, Ogunnaike's collection can be placed in a long tradition of English poets finding inspiration in Islamicate literature. In the 19th century, Edward FitzGerald's *Rubáiyát of Omar Khayyám*—loose translations of quatrains from the Persian poetic tradition—inspired a generation of poets and painters. From an even broader perspective, the history of English literature cannot be isolated from the history of Persian and Arabic love poetry.

After all, the sonnet comes to us from 13th-century Sicilian poets who themselves were influenced by the troubadours of southeast France. While it is not my place to speculate on such matters here, this troubadour poetry seems to bear the influence of the literary cultures of nearby al-Andalus, where Muslim writers had been expressing the soul-shattering potential of love in neatly-packaged rhyming Arabic poems, in sung strophic styles called the *muwashshaḥa* and the *zajal*.

Indeed, around 200 years before the troubadours, the Spanish poet and scholar Ibn Ḥazm presented a courtly love informed by theories of emanation current among Muslim philosophers and students of the science of Sufism. This empowered his Arabic love poetry. The love for an earthly human being brought with it echoes of the eternal longing of the soul to return to its origin.[1] Placing the beloved on not a pedestal but a throne had been a trait of Arabic poetry from at least the time of the rise of ʿUdhrī poetry, that is, in the first century following the life of the Prophet Muhammad. That tradition celebrated a chaste love that centered the pain of the lover and proclaimed that pain to be purifying, virtuous, and beautiful. As decades passed, Arabic and Persian poets further explored the metaphysical dimensions of that love and reverence. Persian Sufi fascination with the story of Layla and Majnun contributed to this development.[2] Over time, in the poetry of Sanāʾī, ʿAṭṭār, Ibn al-Fāriḍ, Rūmī, ʿIrāqī, and the great Ḥāfiẓ, the union between human and divine beloved became complete. Often the reader of these poets cannot tell whether the love in question is for one of God's creatures or for Himself, and in that ambiguity lay the beauty of this poetic style.

Yet history is not what is at stake here. Rather, this collection of devotional poems seems to aim to bring us to apperceive the divine in the most powerful expressions of human love. In that way, Ogunnaike's collection represents a fine example of cultivating the spiritual imagination. Many of us who have grown up in North America have come to agree upon the importance of imagination, a cultural consensus that is a product of Romantic reactions to the stern rationalism that dominated Europe during the Enlightenment.

---

1. James T. Monroe, *Hispano-Arabic Poetry* (New Jersey: Gorgias, 2004) pp. 18-19.
2. Jokha Alharthi, *The Body in Arabic Love Poetry: The ʿUdhri Tradition* (Edinburgh: Edinburgh University Press, 2021) pp. 40-45.

Far before all of this, however, Ibn ʿArabī, the master of Sufi theory and one of the greatest minds of Islamic thought, taught his audience that God could only be known through the imagination and that the imagination would facilitate presence in prayer. Moreover, in his thought, poetry (love poetry in particular) could help heighten the tension that must exist for every human being between a God who is seen and a God who cannot be seen:

> God is not recognized except through that which He has reported about Himself concerning His love for us, His mercy toward us—as well as His compassion, His sympathy, His showing affection, and His coming down in an act of delimitation for that which is His likeness, may He be exalted. We render Him the idol of our eyes in our hearts, in our prayer-niches, and in our imaginations, until it is "as if we see Him." Rather, we *do* in fact see Him in ourselves, for we recognize Him by means of His imparting Himself, not by means of our own consideration. Among us are those who see Him but fail to recognize Him, and yet it is as though He, in turn, has no need for other than Himself: God does not love anyone among the existents except for Himself, for He is the manifest in every beloved to the eye of every lover. And there is nothing in existence except for the lover. Thus the entire cosmos is lover and beloved, and all of it returns to Him, just as He only worships Himself. After all, anyone who worships does so through the imagination of the divinity within him or her, and were it not for that, that person would not worship.[3]

Ibn ʿArabī uncovers a truth that any seeker of God realizes, which is that, at least while bound to the confines of this body, one only sees God through one's own faculties: the spiritual eyes, the heart, and the imagination. The power of that ability—the ability to see God's activities through our imagination—must be cultivated, but using the paradigms that God has provided through revealed wisdom, that is, through "that which He has reported about Himself." For Ibn ʿArabī, poetry was just such a practice. Poetry represented the pinnacle of bringing supersensory meanings into the form of words. Poetry, above all other arts, was a soul-enhancing, visionary venture.

Poetry works because in the reality of the cosmos there is only

3. Muḥyī al-Dīn Muḥammad ibn ʿAlī ibn al-ʿArabī, *al-Futūḥāt al-Makkīyya* (Beirut: Dār Ṣādir, 1968) p. 2:326. My translation.

one Lover and one Beloved, and both are God, as Ibn ʿArabī tells us above. If we, for the duration of a poem, or perhaps even longer, enjoy the privilege of sharing in God's admiration of Himself, then we should be grateful. Poems such as Ogunnaike's—when read in the state of rapture and imagination in which they were written—can open the doors to a hall in which glances and longing translate to the deepest yearning in every human soul to be known, to be seen, and to discover the reality of existence.

Cyrus Ali Zargar
Al-Ghazali Distinguished Professor
University of Central Florida

***

هو

Abū Razīn said, "I asked, 'O Messenger of God, where was our Lord before He created His creatures?' He replied, 'He was in a Cloud, under which there was no wind and above which there was no wind....'"[4]

"The existence of the cosmos was only made manifest in the Breath of the All-Merciful, namely the Cloud."[5]

*

As the blessed Prophet's words indicate, the cloud is connected to the "space" wherein God resides, and which transforms into the rain of mercy (*raḥma*) that pervades all things. As a metaphysical reality, Ibn ʿArabī explains that the primordial Cloud (*ʿamāʾ*) is the ontological basis of the Muhammadan Reality (*ḥaqīqa Muḥammadiyya*) and directly corresponds to the Breath of the All-Merciful (*nafas al-Raḥmān*) within and through which all of God's words—the stuff of the cosmos—are articulated and formed. In its vapor-like state, a cloud is both here and not here, and hence denotes the principle and substance of manifestation which is simultaneously absent and present throughout the created order.

Given the metaphysically symbolic fecundity of the image of the cloud, in traditional Islamic thought it fittingly represents in-between-ness, imagination, flow, and subtlety, as well as creativity, life, and capaciousness. And what discipline can better encapsulate these qualities than poetry? If Sufi poetry with all its linguistic inflections is known for one thing, it is likely its ability to bring abstract and theoretical teachings to life through the art of imaginalization (*tamaththul*), thereby communicating these verities in concrete and supple linguistic forms and images. Imaginalization by its nature communicates absence through presence, meaning through form, and doctrine through practice. As vehicles for imaginalization, Sufi poetry distinctively reveals the intricate layers of subtlety that interpenetrate the human experience, allowing its audiences to participate in that cloud-like nature which is our very witnessing of and immersion in Divine Reality.

4. Tirmidhī, *Sunan*, no. 3394, in *Jamʿ jawāmiʿ al-aḥādīth wa'l-asānīd wa-maknaz al-ṣiḥāḥ wa'l-sunan wa'l-masānīd*, vol. 6 (Vaduz: Jamʿiyyat al-Maknaz al-Islāmī, 2000).

5. Ibn ʿArabī, *al-Futūḥāt al-Makkiyya* (Beirut: Dār Ṣādir, 1968) 2:415.

Oludamini Ogunnaike's remarkable volume of English Sufi poetry is thus aptly entitled *The Book of Clouds*. These poems are a gift to their author and are likewise a gift to his audience, just as rain is a boon to its recipients. These poems revive the barren land of our hearts which have become dried up by scholasticism, selfishness, social media, and secularism. They distinctively draw on the rich traditions of Arabic and Persian Sufi poetry, while also articulating a Sufi vision that speaks to contemporary audiences whose language is English, and whose worldview is shaped by English. Ogunnaike brings his connection to the living tradition of *taṣawwuf* and distinctive accomplishments as a leading scholar and Muslim thinker to bear on each of this volume's poems, demonstrating not only the vitality of Sufism in English but also a profound relationship to and continuation of the entire tradition of Sufi poetry found in every major Islamic language, past and present.

*

Readers of Sufi poems often note their subtle and overt resonances with various Islamic intellectual traditions in general, and the Quran and Hadith—the bases of all Islamic learning and genuine Muslim activity and ways of being—in particular. The poems enshrined in *The Book of Clouds* are no exception. They in many ways form a veritable commentary upon the Islamic tradition in riveting English verses of great sophistication, rhythmic beauty, and even humor, written in our time and for our time, but which transcend all time. Consider, for example, these verses:

> Beware, beware the smiling shaykhs
> with breath more offensive than mace
> Black hearts, white turbans, and two-faced
> sweet speech by pride's poison debased

There is a world of meaning in these lines, and indeed the entire poem is pregnant with subtle allusions to traditional Islamic scriptural passages and sayings of the great Friends of God (*awliyāʾ Allāh*). These lines in particular take us to a traditional trope in Sufi poetry: the distinction between the outward form of things and their inner reality. In the first instance, these lines are a commentary upon Quran 30:7, *They know an outward aspect of the life of this world, but of the next world they are heedless*. There have always been those who seem to know the nature of things but who actually do not. Such claimants are referred to in the Sufi tradition as "knowers of this world" (*ʿulamāʾ al-dunyā*); they stand in stark contrast to those who are "knowers of the next world" (*ʿulamāʾ al-ākhira*).

These "smiling shakyhs" have "breath more offensive than mace," which is to say they can be found in states of constant ascetic practice (their foul breath being an allusion to a famous Prophetic saying concerning fasting); but in truth, there is nothing real about them apart from their outward trappings. Their hearts are black (symbolizing attachment to the world and immersion in sin) and their turbans white, but their hearts should be white (symbolizing detachment from the world and purity of soul) and their turbans black (symbolizing spiritual descent from the Prophet through the *silsila* or initiatic chain of Sufism). They are "two-faced," as opposed to someone whose entire being is turned toward God through *tawajjuh* (attentiveness), and this because of his awareness that God is constantly facing him (an allusion to several Quranic verses, such as Quran 2:115, *Wheresoever you turn, there is the face of God*).

The reference to the "sweet speech" of such un-knowers calls to mind a famous Hadith in which the Prophet speaks of a people who will recite the Quran but whose meanings will not pass their throats. What does pass these un-knowers' throats is the poison of their pride and egoism, which in the end will cause their destruction and ignominy, as the master of the first and the last says, "There is not a single person but that there are two angels with him, grasping him by his reins. If he elevates himself, they pull them back and say, 'O God! Humiliate him.' And if he humbles himself, they say, 'O God! Elevate him.'"[6]

*

One of my favorite poems in this collection, which is very much in line with the tradition of Arabic and Persian Sufi poetry but distinctively unique in English, comes in the form of a "Wine Ode" (*khamriyya*):

6. Translated in Abū Ḥāmid al-Ghazālī, *The Condemnation of Pride and Self-Admiration*, trans. Mohammed Rustom (Cambridge: Islamic Texts Society, 2018) 15.

This life's too hard to live sober
  so drink and try to die a drunk
For heaven's but a hangover
  for those who drink from your mouth's cup

And when I miss your lips I mix
  love's memories with words in verse
To warm my soul with little sips
  and cool the sharp pain of my thirst
So pour love's lightning in my heart
  and grind my bones to gleaming sparks
All dancing like stars on the tides
  my life's shores end where your love starts

If you spent your life for a drop
  that's cheap—it won't have been in waste
And all your life has been for naught
  if you die now without a taste

So all I have's a burning heart
  fed by tears flowing like the rain
Lips scalded by love's tongues of flame
  can never taste death's bitter pain

In trying to explain the significance of these verses I can do no better than to cite two passages, one on drunkenness and the other on love, from the great Persian Sufi master ʿAyn al-Quḍāt:

> Be in the tavern for one month to see what the tavern and the tavern-dwellers do with you! O metaphorical drunkard! Become a tavern-dweller! Come so that we can go along for one moment!
>
> Without the fire, the moth is restless, but in the fire it does not have existence. So long as the moth flutters around the fire of love, it sees the entire world as fire. And when it reaches the fire, it throws itself in its midst. The moth does not know how to differentiate between the fire and other than the fire. Why? Because love itself is all fire.[7]

*

Allow me to end by offering some brief remarks on the poem entitled "Khalwa":

---

7. Translated in Mohammed Rustom, *Inrushes of the Heart: The Sufi Philosophy of ʿAyn al-Quḍāt* (Albany: SUNY Press, 2023) 233 and 235 respectively.

At the peak of my soul's depths
    I sit in silent reverie
The sun above, weather below
    The bright blue breathes in, out of me

These verses bring *The Book of Clouds* to a close, just as the *khalwa* or spiritual retreat brings a wayfarer's interaction with the world of distraction to a close. There is a finality in these verses, both in terms of their placement in the book and in what they are trying to convey: the goal of the spiritual life is to be with God, to be alone with the Alone, which is why the retreat is a *sine qua non* of the spiritual life. Notice, also, how the state the poet finds himself in, in the depths of his retreat, is something of an interstice: between God and the world there is his soul, and between the sun above and the weather below, there is the cloud from which emerges not only this poem but also the very breath that allows the poet to repeat the divine Name in the *khalwa*.

Wa mā tawfīq illā bi'Llāh

Mohammed Rustom
al-Madīna al-Munawwara
24 Dhū'l-Qaʿda 1444

Preface

This diwan, or collection of poems, began with a pilgrimage to Jalal al-din Muhammad Rumi in Konya in 1430/2009. Upon returning, poems started to flow. I had always enjoyed poetry and had even tried my hand at a few poems here and there before this trip, but what came after was qualitatively different: rhymed and metered and born out of reading, reciting, and listening to the Qur'an and Sufi poetry in English translation, in Arabic, and in Persian. The result is an experiment in grafting the classical forms of these traditions—the qasida, the ghazal, the ruba'i, and the qit'a—into the soil of my English, inflected and enriched as it is with Yoruba, Arabic, and Afro-diasporic accents and angles of attack to the language of *The Cloud of Unkowing*, John Donne, Emily Dickinson, Gerard Manley Hopkins, Langston Hughes, Bob Marley, Fela Kuti, Lucille Clifton, Bill Withers, and MF DOOM. For example, the poem entitled "Qasidat al-Madh" that concludes the collection's opening section, is written in the Kāmil meter of Arabic prosody (*Mutafā'ilun Mutafā'ilun Mutafā'ilun Mutafā'ilun*) and is modeled on the famous pre-Islamic Qasida of 'Antara ibn Shaddād. To paraphrase Rumi, "Say it in English even if Persian and Arabic sound better, Love itself has a hundred other languages," or as Hafiz instructs, "Hafiz, [English] and Arabic are the same in this work, tell the story of love in the language that you know."

But the poems of this diwan are not a literary exercise, they were born from a kind of inward necessity and pressure to work out grief, bewilderment, longing, love, delight, gratitude, and insights in body, mind, and soul at once, which is to say, in poetry. Good poetry moves us from the depths of our hearts to the tips of our hairs, and its medium is our very living breath. Poetry is an attempt to sing what can't be said but must be expressed. These poems are meant to be read and heard aloud; they're meant to be like clouds of smoke that you pull in and puff out yourself and contemplate, hence one meaning of the title. Clouds are liminal realities between Heaven and Earth that connect the two with rain and lightning, life and wonder, shade and light, beauty and power, and that's what good poetry can do and be. The poems are mostly untitled, in keeping with the conventions of diwan poetry, being known by their first lines, an index of which can be found at the end of the book. Some poems are formatted with what might seem to be unusual spacing, meant to mark pauses to help the reader catch the rhythm of each verse. Each poem begins with a bolded capital letter, and they are organized thematically, beginning with a devotional prologue of poems in praise of the Prophet Muhammad, the Virgin Mary, and various Sufi masters, a section of rend (gangster / rascal lovers of God) poems in the style of Hafiz and al-Hallaj, a section of poems on language and poetry itself, a section of ghazals (most of which adhere to the classical form), and a section of elegies, mostly in a modified qasida form, written to mourn the deaths of so many I have loved from near and afar. But all of these poems are about love, which is to say, they are about God. As Ibn al-'Arabi wrote, "I have a Beloved whose name is that of all those who have a name." Or as Dante wrote, "All my thoughts always speak to me of love." Or better, as Rumi said:

> Since your love was kindled in my heart
> Apart from your love, all that I have has burned
> My heart put reason and study and books on the shelf
> And was taught poetry and ghazals and quatrains

> "If not for You, I would not know Love, if not for Love, I would not know You"
> But shh... I'm busy falling in Love with You, O Majestic, My Beautiful

مقدمة

Prologue

You're the lightning in the clouds
and you're the falling rain
You, the blazing light and heat
that make all rise again

You're the cloud, the sun, and shade
You, the ground it falls upon
You, light's coolness in each eye
You, whose sight rights every wrong

You, the cloud of perfumed breath
within which all worlds' words take shape
The start of love, the end of death
our refuge and our one escape

The meeting place of the two seas
Your body binds Infinity
You, who are more I than me
Your knotted locks have set me free

You are love's ocean's waterfall, all beauty's charms descend in you
though it seems too good to be true, all of my longings end in you

The music from beyond the skies, the sweetness growing in the earth
wind's sighs and wisdom, I find in the love notes that He sends in you

The sunlight falling on the ground that starts dust and drops' desperate dance
is but a shadow of your glance, every last joy ascends in you

My heart felt like it swallowed stones, a singing bird lost in salt dunes
with broken wings, without a home, my tears and tears all mend in you

Once all alone and seeking proofs inside of dreams as firm as clouds
you woke me up, tore off the roof—it seems all veils do rend in you

All I have read, all my ink's lines, all signs between the two vast blues
though I have tried and searched, they can't compare to what He's penned in you

My thorny heart burst into bloom, drunk at the mere mention of you
beyond imagination's reach, the mercy He extends in you

Not even bound by boundlessness, each shackle and limitation
each heaven and its reflection, I find my soul transcends in you

The wonders of this wide, wide world and the next too, all pale next to
the humble might and silent light of what I apprehend in you

A dew drop that holds all the worlds, the deep inkwell of your pupil
without color contains all words—colors' delights all blend in you

Like light inside your pearly eyes, sunbeams in ocean's prisms' dew
all of my chains, all prison bars, all of my thoughts do bend in you

Your beauty has blinded the sun, and like the chattering parrots do
Eden grew green in envy of the garden that He tends in you

Like Arabic lips' gymnastics, like His Name and my last breath too
and like the end of every clue, all my beginnings' end in you

The wind beneath the mighty wings of Sulayman's throne and kingdom
how wondrous that all that he brings is in your hand, depends on you

He's everything and I'm nothing, how far apart are false and true
how is it that we both seem to have found a mirror and friend in you?

Don't leave me to myself for one instant
if you blink, I'll vanish without remnant

Because I know without you I just can't...
my own thoughts I repent and all recant

I just can't trust myself when I'm with you
I'm but a fog that your light burns, shines through

When your beautiful face gives my eyes' sight
and draws the night from day, and day from night

Drag me back to you, joyful through the stars
and past all place to where only you are

Unswerving, my gaze fixed on you always
let me float through these fading dreams with ease

In footsteps of the shadowless orphan
whose praise is my heart's flame, joy's endorphins

Whose beauty's past the moon's and still more than
whose light did all walls into wide doors rend

A prayer upon him, family, and poor friends
and peace like musk spreading on the four winds

A prayer from You to You, no break, nor end
a prayer that makes the heart-sore soar and then

More blessings, peace upon him pour and send
whose poverty is the glory of men

Who is for us heaven's own door and end
who's closer than ourselves, more than a friend

The sky's veils his ascent all tore and rent
by his descent broken hearts' cores did mend

Upon God's rope that has never worn thin
be all blessings and poems' offerings

Upon him for all time, at each instant
as long as there abides love's sparks' remnants

The full moon floats like a pearl of your praise
    in sky's page blackened by ink of your praise

A drop of your milk left all the worlds dazed
    the stars winking drunk, 'cause they love your praise

My pen writes light on the midnight sea's skin
    mine's scintillating because of your praise

My heart holds heaven and handles hell's flames
    without pain, wrapped in the gloves of your praise

The trees are all reaching up for your grace
    composing and spreading leaves of your praise

My book—burned all black and stained by my sins—
    was turned to mirrors by doves of your praise

The sun's but a drop from your honey face
    and galaxies are bees that buzz your praise

Because you climbed up beyond time and space
    each breath, every place is full of your praise

Stronger than the sun's, gentler than the moon's
    your light's all sight, we're all rays of your praise

Only the Most High could your love appraise
    what's there left to say that's above your praise?

Your beard's night glistens with stars and dawn's gleams
    the heavens' are but echoes of your praise

Because of your praise, all's swallowed in light
    nothing shines so bright-black as does your praise

The secret to all Sulayman's kingdom,
    his wealth and wisdom, it all was your praise

Although speech can't reach the half of your praise
    all time can never run out of your praise

The moon's pearl split from our love of your praise
    strung on days' spiral necklace of your praise

Your glances are lances of bright black mercy
sheathed in banners of brilliant majesty
Your pupils, dark springs of all life's beauties
and your mouth's the source of all mysteries

And lo, but for you, my life would be lack
and so, without you, my love's just abstract
Although, due to you, I'm true to my pact
by you, I broke through all bonds and all facts

I'd lost myself, searching the world for my eyes
then you appeared, and in your mirror, I found mine
Your iris, your pupils, the whites of your eyes
are the heart, and essence, and light within mine

Black ink swelled up from your deep pupils' wells
and flowed in patterns, across your eyes' page
Your lashes are thousands of shining black quills
that write with light throughout each and every age

And no one has ever seen your like or kind
and no one has ever encompassed your sight
To know one who bewilders all hearts and minds
two bow's length, your two brows, the niche and the light
we leap through, and come in, leaving all behind

Your glances are lances of bright black mercy
sheathed in banners of brilliant majesty

You took the lightning from the skies
    and planted it inside my heart
you filled my chest with burning sighs
    that taught my eyes the raincloud's art

Your truth extinguished all my lies
    your light cast away all my dark
my doubts scatter like swarms of flies
    before the flood that lifts your ark

And when the knife had reached the bone
    and when my heart had reached my throat
when I was lost and all alone
    you showed my feet the way back home

My soul was on the brink of death
    you saved me with your Christ-like breath
I cried 'till I had nothing left
    you soothed me with the gift of Seth

I rolled my soul like die with death
    you caught me in your wisdom's net
And taught my spirit how to rest
    on high, in mountain eagles' nests

Forgive me for my long absence
    I'm unused to this abstinence
but since you are my senses six
    I never leave your sweet presence

I know that your heart won't forget
    my own for getting infrequent
My heart revived just by your scent
    and near, far into exile sent

The earth has gone around again
    the sun and moon resume their place
Though brilliant, both of them still seem
    but shadows of your brighter face

I praise you for the sake of one
who was before the clay was baked
Who drowns the seas and folds the skies
and in whose steps the mountains quake

I praise you for the sake of one
before whom all the stars prostrate
Who rose in light before the sun
whose tears turned hell into a lake
Whose rose holds heavens in its folds
who carries all souls in his wake

You know my soul, my wretched state
accept the words of this poor rake
Here is my heart, my hopes, my fate
here is my thirst for you to slake
Here are my aches and my complaints
and what you give is what I'll take
please ask your Lord, by your namesake:

For mercy and intercession,
forgiveness for my transgressions
I just want to behold His face
and be held near His placeless place

By your light, I read His praise
in your night, I see His trace
By this sight, my soul is saved
by the right of His great Name
Please ransom me before I'm late
O my star, my moon, my shaykh

The king of martyrs' tragedy
became my poor soul's victory
Your exile in the far sunset
broke dawn in my heart's dark lament
The setting of my moon's crescent
came from your bright sun's swift ascent
The bright lights of the orient
thawed winter shadows' discontent
And from my drunken reveries
revived my heart to ecstasies
Beyond all bliss, all fantasy
is love's flame that you lit in me
Oppression filled my heart with blood
but you turned my blood into wine
The flood of grace that you called down
lifted us up beyond all time

You split the seas, and split my heart
and polished bright what once was dark
My soul's dark stains are all washed bright
within gleams of your eyes' black light
Your tears and whispered prayers by night
quickened my clay, restored my sight
I'm less than dust, but on your breeze
the golden sun's rays carry me
A grain of sand gripped by your tide
will dive to depths' eternity

Maryam

The quiet gasp before the song
    the gentle touch that bests the strong
The silent breath that holds all words
    the sweet birdcalls that bring the dawn

Your perfume lends wine its wisdom
    and gives the night its mystery
And Nature, her secret rhythms
    your darkness makes my pale eyes see

The night flower that birthed its earth
    the moon forms petals ‘round your face
Crowned with the sun, adorned with stars
    the heavens spin in your embrace

So pure that scandalous you seem
    like light so bright that it looks black
The dark ocean teeming with gleams
    that from these false shores calls me back

Gentle mother, mighty mercy
    meaning of my melodies
Cover me with your warm mantle
    take me in your arms, Lady

And all that’s fair within this world
    white stars and golden harmonies
All praise you just because they are
    sewn from threads of your soul’s beauty

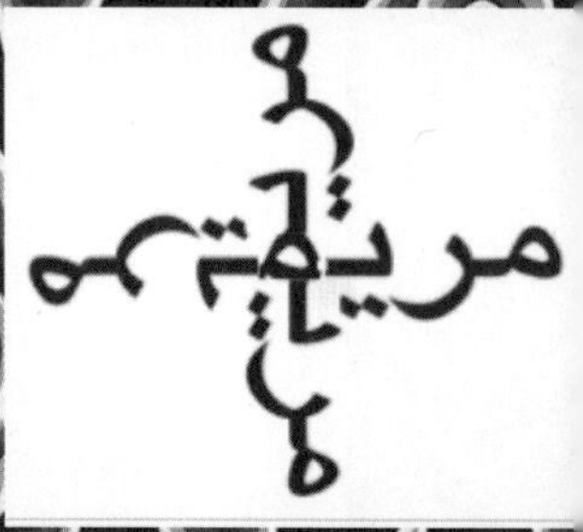

Humaythra

Her eyes are black from all the nights
she's stolen from men's sleep
Her lips are red from all the blood
that for her face they weep
And if you could see the brave hearts
she's skewered on her lashes
You'd understand our state and want
to join us in our madness

But just as hope was fleeing me
I caught her scent from love's alley
And followed it to desert winds
that spoke of my love's hidden friend

I crossed mountains and desert plains
lonely green trees and sandy graves
in search of the house of your slave
who welcomed me, taught me her ways

He gave me a shawl of her scent
and a cup with her face in it
Drinking revived my dying strength
and guided me into love's tent

I watched her move behind the stars
and through my veins, so near, so far
My home is where her people are
so bless the folk of Humaythra

She wound all my scattered, split hopes
into one end, like my life's rope
Then burned them all to bind them fast
and sealed them up with her mouth's kiss
To pass me through her needle's eye
and sew her dress with me tonight
I dance through life, towards death gladly
in the tracks of al-Shadhili

Bamba

The moon fell in the desert's lap
its dark dunes birthed a brilliant white
His face burned bright black from love's flames
the longing of the depth of night
A blackness pure, so dazzling
its shadow is the morning light
The sun squints at his face, blinking
straining so hard to catch his sight
His dark face so intense and bright
he had to shroud himself in white

Like clouds veiling the heavens' gleams
that makes them both hidden and seen
Like scents upon the morning breeze
the echo of a midnight dream

The dazzling dark flows through his veins
like ink pregnant with poetry
And fills his eyes and skin with verses
teeming with love's mysteries

How do you see us from your seat
beneath the shade of heaven's tree?
The baobabs must look like lightning
flashing from the earth and falling
Skies must seem a fickle frailty
whirling 'round your finger's ring

The shadow of the shade of God
leaping from your pure heartstrings
Floods the dry and dusty lands
sweeping the old bones along
Dancing in the secret rapture
of the silence of your song

Baye Niasse

A garden of light in a desert of flame
because of your love, the earth burns the same

Who knew human clay could hold such fire
your words' breath makes love's flames leap up higher

If not for the flood that flowed from your pen
that flowed from Kosi, out to the world's end

If not for the flood that poured from your eyes
and ran rivers to the beloved's side
We'd all be burnt up by your lightning sighs
but still this love burns us out from inside

If not for this passion you lit in our hearts
we'd all be lost, drowned in your brilliant dark

O where have you gone, Baye, and what have you seen?
and what have you tasted, behind all our dreams?
And what of the rest of us caught in between
the sunset's last gasp and sunrise's first gleams?

When the Messenger comes, who's his bright shadow?
who's that who comes floating behind him like snow?

Who's back there, black, gleaming,
just like his eyelashes?

Baye Niasse is, Baye Niasse is,
Baye Niasse is, Baye Niasse is...

Istiʿādha

In your lap I seek refuge, from all of my pain
 from all of life's pleasures, and all of its games
From all that I've lost, and all I have gained
 from all of my efforts, and all of their strains
From heaven's bright gardens, and from hell's dark flames
 from space and from time, and all they contain
From everything that either waxes or wanes
 from everything that's been touched by my stain
From all words and all names and all need to explain
 and from you, all else is just vanity, feigned

Qasidat al-Madh

Did the poets leave room for one like me?
To declaim your praise in my ‘Ajami?

All the world rushing to Tayba’s shade trees,
in a crush like the Judgement day coming

Plucking petals from that garden gently
tossing them back like a second blooming

What have I to bring to this gathering?
—broken pearls and heart, a worn-out body

Like a falling leaf on the evening breeze,
my soul’s sorrow rides on this melody,

The wind howling in every dry wadi,
like the scars running down my sunken cheeks

Like doves cooing under the moon’s soft beams,
singing our pain, cause we’re to weak to weep

I recall last night, your moon came to me
like the sun burning through my cloudy dreams

And the morning broke with its cold white streaks
running through my hair, like ashes, stars’ gleams

And with Time’s frost fast creeping over me
with life unwinding ever more quickly

I watch myself sinking into quicksands,
In ignomy, agony, anomie

Then a smile flashed like midnight lightning,
igniting a fire deep inside of me

How could I hold on to a pulsing coal?
my heart, burning, lost in your mystery

Now I search for it in your beauty’s sea,
across deserts of your bright majesty

How can I go on when my sins are chains,
weighing me down, wounding so heavily?

Like the tentacles of a giant squid,
pulling me into the abyss, murky

How can I go on through hours like concrete?
When everything rises menacingly?

And the thorns all tear at my hopes and shred
all my pride and rip through my dignity

And the sky is filled with the missiles' dread,
like the meteors for nosy jinni

And my body's filled with regret and pains
and the horizons, filled with enemies

And the trials fall all around like rain,
and my friends all fall or turn tail and flee

And the earth is shaking beneath our feet
and the floods are sweeping away cities

How can I go on? I can barely see
but for flashes of your bright eyes' beauty

How could I not dive straight into this sea?
With your lovely scent always beckoning?

How could I not run to you when I see
all the beauties and terrors around me

Are but your shadows and their boundaries,
and each step I take, you come fast, running?

With death's icy breath on my back and with
the Fire's flames licking around my feet

How can I walk this molten path scorching?
My soles hotter still from my soul's burning

How could I not race towards you, my safety
What is there to seek but your company?

Your glances' harpoons have long since speared me,
Don't spare me, just drag my soul out to sea

What are bee stings, but the spice of honey?
What are thorns except petals' harmony?

What is this mirage, but a chance to see
through the limits of all infinity?

I remember you in days, struggling,
and I think of you through nights troubling

The gun's muzzle flash, echo thundering
like your glance and your whispers, humbling

And I wanted to kiss all the lightning
like your smile, swift and devastating

I remember you in calamities
even as they wound and dismember me

With guns to my head, knives at my kidneys,
my cheek's on your chest, sleeping peacefully

My rest and repose in blows' destiny
is thinking of you thinking about me

Fate's lances, like straws, drink my life freely,
I lift my wounds' cups to your lips gladly

Loving you is such a strange alchemy:
the more you I see, then the less I'll be

For how often have you healed a body?

For how many hearts are you remedy?

For how many souls did you intercede?
And how many poor slaves have you set free?

The whole world fell in love with your beauty,
gazelles and the clouds, lizards and the trees

While the whole world's living inside your dream
the secret of all, all's in you complete

Truth is, you're the truth, whom Truth loves dearly,
And all loves are yours, yours is all glory

Yet how many nights did you stand lonely?
Flying through the veils no one else could see?

Limits of perfection, humanity,
you left all behind and returned humbly

Like the circle of your own letter meem,
Nearer than two bows, joining seen, unseen

If you want to praise him in poetry,
try to use your cup to empty the seas

All the words of all tongues' dictionaries
are just incense for your lovely body

And all languages that are, were, will be:
robes too short to cover up your beauty

So here we conclude, inadequately,
trusting in your kindness and clemency

These pearls of yours I've strung imperfectly—
please accept my graceless love graciously

And make it healing for my progeny
And a blessing for one who hears or reads

Fulfilling all of our wants and needs,
even as your rain fills up all the seas

I made its verses number sixty-three,
like the years in time of our dear Hadi

Even as your soul lights eternity,
time's an echo of your reality

So I join God and angels' harmony
Praying peace and blessings eternally

Upon the essence of nobility,
the light of all sights who's more me than me

And upon his beautiful family,
and then those who follow them faithfully

And all those for whom he is a mercy,
under his vast cloak's generosity

As long as doves sing on the morning breeze,
and a lover asks sleepless, sheepishly,

"Did the poets leave room for one like me?
To declaim your praise in my 'Ajami?"

رندیّات

Rindiyyat

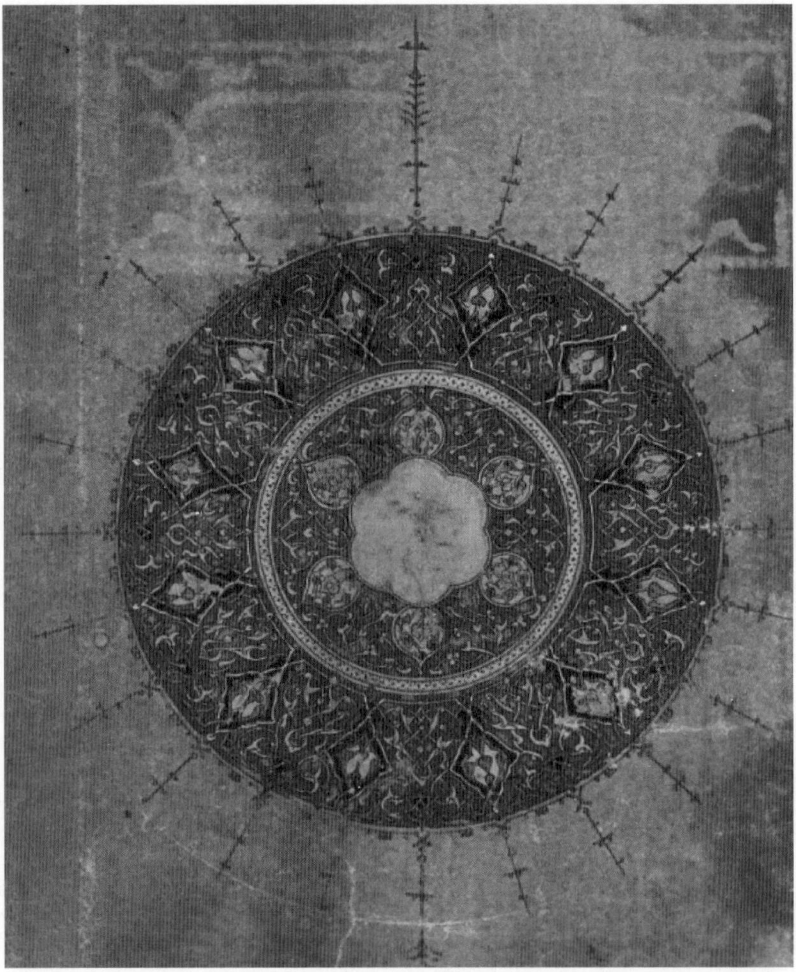

لا اله الا الله
محمّد رسول الله

Shahada

Of this alone my faith consists:
There's no sweetness but your lips
And I know this from your kiss
So kiss me in remembered bliss
Make me forget that I exist.

Your eyes peer out behind my own
The earth's core is a spinning sun
There's a heart within my heart
That holds the world beyond this one

We are tears, but no ocean can hold us
    Just dust, but more weighty than boulders
What broke the sky and the earth's shoulders
    Is what makes our hearts burn and eyes smolder
Fresh as buds, but than time, we are older
    Soft snowflakes but we're harder than soldiers
We dew drops grab the sun's hair and hold her
    Until she returns what we owe her
Though this life's hard as winter and colder,
    To the nightingales we are all roses
Though this night's long—they've shackled and sold us,
    When dawn's breeze blows, we're those who arose first
Sulayman knows these spells and all those versed
    So your poetry's cursed, and your prose worse
Most men who break this silence are posers
    What we've tasted has sewn closed our mouth's mirth
Those who know can read well our woe's smirk
    We are tears but no ocean can hold us

Love

At last, a cure for all my pains
    alas, it's pain without a cure
A sickness that treats all disease
    a ravishing that made me pure

A wound that heals all other scars
    a wine that made my head sober
An ocean that dried all my tears
    a birth that meant my life's over

I fell ill heartfirst in this love
    there's neither hope nor remedy
A prison that broke all life's bars
    my friend, please don't let me be free

A poison that made me immune
    to health and all I once thought best
A death in life and life in death
    came to me on your gentle breath

I've never seen my love wear clothes
she wraps herself in her hair's light
That flutters in winds as she flows
in brilliance darker than the night

My mind melts to sweat on her skin
like snowflakes o'er a dancing flame
Each drop, a world enfolded in,
glides, glistening round her beauty's frame

Her clothing is her nakedness
-but when we kiss, we close our eyes
and nakedness is her clothing
-as truth is only told by lies

All that I gain, I forefeit
my disguises, all self-portraits
All I've tried to hide is opened
seeds' secrets are spilled by orchids

My love is wholly without shame
and I likewise am shameless
Because we are each other's clothes
we're naked still, yet blameless

Your two lips bind beauty's Qur'an
    your eyelashes are long koans
there're sutras written on your skin
    each breath and every gasp a hymn
your heartbeat is a sacred drum
    where all sounds go, where life comes from
your hands are two golden icons
    that cast my bones' divination
my soul's the sky, and you're the sun
    between our breaths and our poems
—between them, though our hearts are one—
    are meadows where the gazelles run

Heart-wrecked and diving deep headfirst
    into sky's cloudy sea
Is what it feels like when your eyes
    look up and then see me

I lost my head, just like a ball
    that rolled into your street
Your beauty hit me like a car
    and knocked earth from my feet

The maze of life's full of dead ends
    love's endless path's no start nor bends

Beyond, behind, before, between,
    this love flows deep beneath all dreams
The ocean of reality
    fills up all streams and bursts the seams
Binding our words to what they mean
    this love is more than this life seems

My soul melts and drips from my eyes
    onto paper in blurry lines
And spilling through my keyboard's cracks
    sparks my mind and my mem'ry fries

Bless all that survived my grief's flood
    but cursed's all not burnt by your love

The maze of life's too bent to mend
    but love's steep path's no start nor end

Love is a sea without shore, I'm the shore
    Beauty is all, I'm the less that is more
Bubbles reach for sky from ocean's dark floor
    Raindrops and light dive and in the deep, soar
In the world's fruit, we're the juice and the core
    Your face lights the world, we're its windows' door

When you race to me, then I walk to you
    My hand raised to knock, your hand pulls me through

It's only from you back to you I flee
    I guard you from you, you save me from me
Have you ever swum within waveless seas?
    A wave without sea is thought but not seen
I'm in the ocean, the ocean's in me
    See her, you see me, and it's she who sees
Love's sky set all my horizons' bounds free
    My soul's Sulayman's cloud rug on the breeze

My soul's bound by each strand of hair
    So when, haughty, you toss your head
It tears my body limb from limb
    And scatters me for birds like bread

You stabbed me but you took the knife
    Time came and took the wound
Now all I have left from that night,
    A scarred face like the moon

The moon blushes and burns to tar
    From your bows' darts and your lips' kiss
Arrows bring prey down from afar
    For rose-sheathed dagger's close finish

You've tortured me so long, I fear
    I've even craved death's hard embrace
To taste the sweet salt of your tears
    Now falling gently on my grave

My epitaph is on your teeth
    your rose lips are my funeral wreath
It's beautiful to die beneath
    the tender blossoms of your speech
Your hair, my prayer mat and my shroud
    envelop me in your dark cloud
I know now why the crickets sing
    the music of the falling leaves
So let the sun abandon me
    your shadow's all the light I need

Her full moon and midnight tresses
    left me wasted like a crescent
Loving leaves me unrepentant
    every wink's a fatal sentence
My dignity's all rent to shreds
    still smiling, she leaves me for dead
My love's a last leaf hanging silent
    blood-red in the wind, defiant

My room, it has two windows
    But the sunlight won't shine through
I found a leak in this roof
    That my soul's got to rise through
My heavy sins are many
    And my saving virtues few
The world has many colours
    But all I see is blue
Your mouth is full of answers
    But all I want's the truth
I've tasted plenty raptures
    But all I want is you

You forged these chains and set me free
    I'm your dream, you're my memory
Don't forget me, I beg you please
    my darkness, light, health and disease

My love is yours, so yours is mine
    so lift my ore out of this mine
Don't leave me shrouded in my mind
    love flows behind the clouds of time

Only my death will end our war
    my perfections stain your faults
My waves will crash upon your shore
    until your rocks become my salt

Hide me in your mouth till I'm sweet
    like your sugar mountains of teeth
Let me be a breath of your speech
    my heart is where your two lips meet

A river and a tulip tree
    lightning and its melody
Like truth beyond fantasy
    here and now, not you, not me

The whole world fits inside my head
    —a small price just to be with you

Hearts hold God's throne and heaven too
    —I gambled them just to kiss you

For what are this world and the next
    except a place to not miss you?

And what are time and fate except
    the lucky chance of meeting you?

It's true, I'm myself only when
    I haply find myself in you

Or when I'm smacked out of my mind
    —that's nothing next to seeing you

All life's burdens, facing my end
    —light work compared to loving you

How strange is the lover's creed
    wherein repentance is a sin
These holy places scream "get out!"
    while dens of sin say "come on in..."

While branches fight, their roots embrace
    these rind-chewers spit in your face
Of that sweet juice, they have no taste
    kernel's fruit with love's sugar laced

Beware, beware the smiling shaykhs
    with breath more offensive than mace
Black hearts, white turbans, and two-faced
    sweet speech by pride's poison debased

Only the *rends* who drink disgrace
    can put all in their proper place
Can rend the veils of our mistakes,
    rend'ring rare justice commonplace

Only with them is your soul safe
    with its slim waist and bright moon face
With them, nothing can go to waste
    only their hearts can bear our weight

These headless horsemen on night rides
    hang hundreds of Hallaj's high
Lights burning bright across the sky
    to guide us to the other side

Don't give your hand to those white snakes
    of bloodshot eyes, and soul-stained face
they feed upon your hope and joy
    and give you grief's wounds in their place

Love and good name can't share a space
    like darkness in fire's embrace
Like angels chasing out demons
    love rushes in when you're effaced

Leave them and come sit in the ruins
    where soft hearts like petals are strewn
On souls love's tempered more than steel
    real humans, polished and rough-hewn

How strange is the lovers' creed
    wherein repentance is a sin
Alarm bells tell us to come out
    while broken hearts' beats beckon in

Paradise is for the pious
    Your lips, for those still on fire
If, once, you passed by the righteous
    God, I swear, they'd start a riot
This piety is for your friends
    But lovers start where goodness ends

Some build homes in paradise
    Others make theirs in verse
My palace is between your lips
    Heaven's within your earth

All of my sin is worship, and all my worship's sin
    If everywhere I see your lips, how could I not fall in?
But your face is beyond the sun, so how could I kiss you?
    But if all lips are yours, then I wonder who's kissing whose?
So every time I try to kiss, I trip and I miss you
    But your love swerves all of my slips, your aim alone is true

Theology's pornography,
Philosophy's fan fiction
I don't want to talk, I want
Your lips, not their description

I'm a dirty little boy
But you can't confuse me
I'll dance on the heads of kings
When crowned with your beauty

I don't know who you are
Or even what I am
But whatever's between us
Has me firmly in its hand

Forget about your poetry,
forget music, and dance
This love is not a game, my friend
it's real life, not romance
It's serious as death again
and twice as hard to stand
Your life is but the bargained price
for stealing just a glance
Your life is but the bargained price
for stealing just a glance

Since my eyes fell on your beauty
swarms of evil eyes pursued me
I swatted them away like flies
but your one glance shot right through me
They seek my blood, I seek your heart
because you stole mine so cruelly

Planted 'neath your balcony
wat'ring flowers with my eyes
Chasing storm clouds with my sighs
too weak to live, too strong to die

Waiting for your glance to fall
on me like a guillotine
Setting body and head free
from this wishful, hopeless dream

This love is not a river,
it's an ocean of fire
A broad desert of ceaseless sighs,
wide skies of vast desire

And there's no way get across,
it's too hard to swim down
So keep away from the edge or
plunge in and burn and drown!

The candle flame has hitched a ride
on this moth bound for the sun
Climbing moonbeams to your face
your eyes become my drop's ocean

Don't blame me for this smoke
  it was you who lit the fire
Don't complain of the heat
  it's my body on the pyre

It's your fault that I hope, my dear
  and you caused all this pain
Sweet as it is, please stop playing—
  I can't take this and the blame

I dreamed that I kissed you
  and I prayed I'd never wake
I heard that I missed you
  and my life I tried to take
But found that you'd beat me to it
  my life was yours before I knew it

Don't leave me stumbling in the dark
  with flashes of your lightning smile
Please light my path and guide my ark
  have mercy on a heart beguiled!

Let me be your veil, my love
  kissing your lips with every breath
Let me be your hair, above
  your bright eyes, glinting dark as death

Your eyes are blinding eclipses
  within these magic ellipses
See all that was, will be, and is
  but only if you hush—listen!

It seems like I'm your shadow
  I can't even get away
So cast me anywhere you will
  all I can do is sway

Where you fly is where I run
  and where you stop is where I'm through
Waiting for high noon to come
  and return me back to you

Beneath your feet is where I'm from
    between your finger and your thumb
My heart is spinning, sick, struck dumb
    by this love, what I—you've become

Forget about your poetry,
    forget music, and dance
This love is not a game, my friend
    It's real life, not romance

It's serious as death again
    and twice as hard to stand
Your life is but the bargained price
    for stealing just a glance
Your life is but the bargained price
    for stealing just a glance

I met myself before the dawn
With just a gown of starlight on

I am rain, and you're my cloud
I fall for, from, and to you

I am song and you're my breath
I flow out and back to you

I am sugar, you're my tongue
Life is sweet only with you

I'm an ear and you're music
My canyons were made for your streams
I'm a kiss from your two lips
You're memory and I'm your dream

I am light, and you're eyes' sight
I look out from you to you

You're my ground and horizons
I walk on from you to you

I am sea and you are sky
Within our one blue I fly

To where there is no you nor I
Only a cloud without a sky

Come look, see your light peeking through
    my eyes, my worn soul bleeding you

Come pierce my eyes' two pearls and watch
    the two seas pour out seeking you

My two parched lips will only part
    for yours, in hopes of sneaking through

For our lips, like their lovers too
    must part only for speaking truth

And stars, like sugar scattered in
    sky's veil are your sight leaking through

For there is only here's disguise
    your dreams play hide and seek with you

This whole life's just a game of catch
    you throw just when I, sleeping, threw

Your light shrinks time to fine raisins
    your wine in my brain's seeping through

When hearts kiss you in every taste
    don't waste your time critiquing views

Somehow this pawn found your board's edge
    at dawn, he'll fly as we king you

All's one, but all is many too
    bright mirrors, the pronouns three sing true

Love leaves me wasted, wipes me out
    stops me from thinking, speaking two

The seas get drunk on your moonlight
    my eyes drink skies like fleeting dew

Your love comes banging on death's drum
    limbs quaking, my heart's beating too

My silence waxes eloquent:
    I wane, your crescent breaking through

All pearls are pierced by love for you
    hanging from necks, ears, speaking clues

When on your whispers breaking dawn
    Sulayman flies, clouds weeping too

Then oceans turn to mirrors of tears
    and stars all fall in streaking blue

All loves, in every longing heart,
    all desire's burning, seeking you

شاعريّات

Ars Poetica

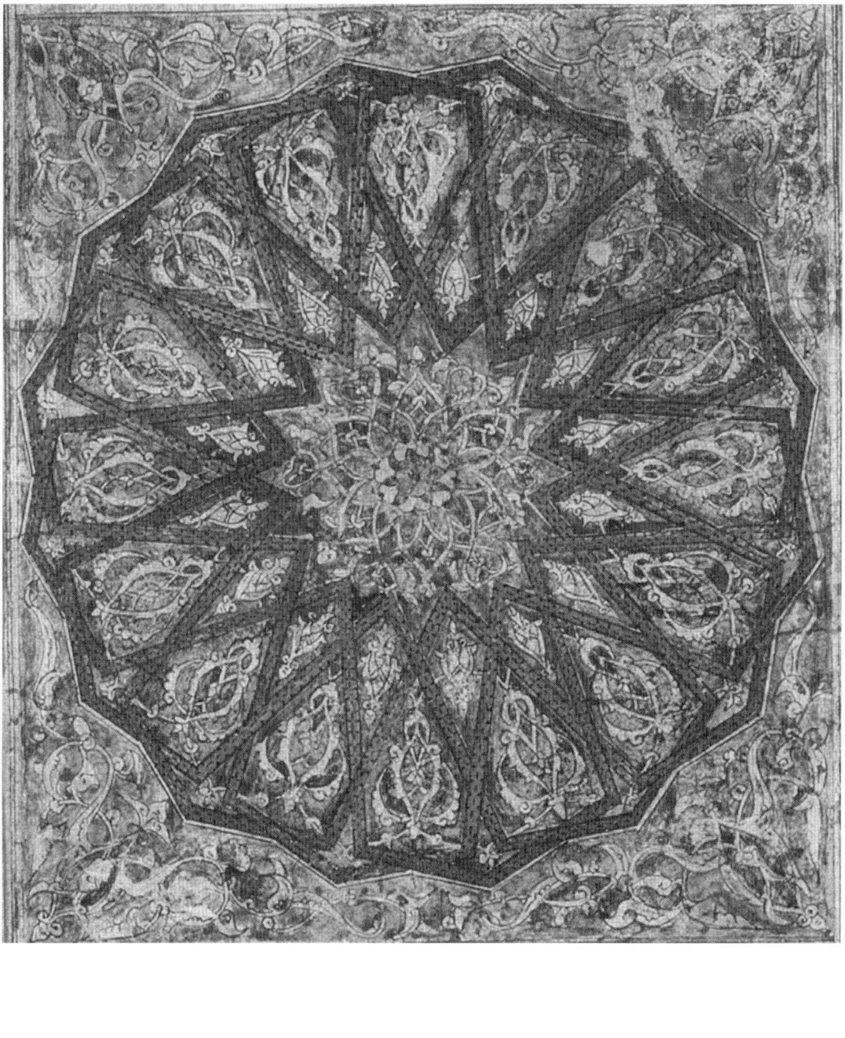

I sketch a few black clouds upon a page
and watch its thinness grow deeper than sky
My musk ink makes mirrors of her moon-white face
and in this dark ocean, I drown and fly

So will you walk with me tonight?
Leave cloudy footprints in the sky?
Come hang your dreams out up to dry
Let go, let me teach you to fly

I'll fill the white night of your pages
With black stars, dark lights of sages
I'll scribble rivers, not equations
We'll wash our words and become nameless

Last night, your love shook me awake
    and threw me on the beach
Your vast ocean of meaning roared
    crushing the sands of speech
The star-grains twinkled up above
    mirrors of pearls in the deep
And what I saw but could not say,
    beyond my mind's short reach:

Within each, the all, and within the all, no breach
    Every thing is everything, but you're no thing to seek
And withholding nothing, you're wholly no thing to each
    So this holy nothing is all I have learned to teach
Like my tears, you walk upon the deserts of my cheek
    While I'm nothing but a click between your tongue and teeth
Your black light is beyond all sight, your kisses beyond speech
    The taste of every song takes me right back where your lips meet

Beyond the din of screeching pens
    between the lines' definitions
Lies what our words can't quite pen in
    truth without shore roars like oceans

A bee seeds the flowers
    the birds sing the trees
These words that you speak are
    what we are and breathe

Not all who sing are poets
    and not all poets sing
Truth is—beyond and yet within
    the wind stirred up by wings—

Within all songs, silence is found—
    loud flower's sky and quiet ground
The black of night, the bright of day
    in your eyes' vibrant depths are drowned—

And so Love hides inside my poems
    to kiss your lips as you recite them
Falling into a place beyond time
    beyond space where I am yours and you're mine

My garden of verses
was burned by your fire
Rows of blossoms turned to
fall leaves' wild desire

The spring of your glance is
what songs do to dances
These rainbows of senses
spell our hearts' romances

How wondrous that all this
sprung from pupils' blackness
And how strange it all fits
within this part of it

How can heaven's sea depths
be found in mirror's flatness?
My heart's dew drop holds best
What's past skies' black vastness

This well drinks words' shoreless
oceans dry and formless
My blood's hot ink, wordless
does far better express
Greater in a world less
the form of emptiness
All of our existence
reformed by nothingness

This love knows no excess
as tasting needs no guess
As passion needs no rest,
filling both easts and wests
These mirrors of polished breaths
forged in love's heaving breasts
And hung 'round your slim neck
like pearls of precious sweat

Can see further than scopes
on high volcanoes' slopes
They split atoms and coax
secrets from tiny motes

A nail knocks out a nail
    and love replaces love
Can words replace a wail?
    my love is your love's veil

When kings enter a town
    they raze it to the ground
When your beauty stands up
    my idols all fall down

And if your love should come again
    uprooting all my thoughts and pens
I'll forget all save you, my friend
    your bright virtues and my dark sins

My soul's flame dances, twirls within
    your breath, circling, bewildering
My heart's leaf flutters on your whims
    like Sulayman upon the wind

In this bright barque of my dark craft
    I'll make my way to your far shore
Where your shade burns it all to ash
    and drowns us in our thirst for more

Upon the pages of the sky,
    you write your verses in sunlight
Then with the wind, them I recite
    to summon beauties of the night

But on the papers' sharpened edge
    is where you seat all of your friends
On beds as fine as blades of hair
    is where lovers meet you, their end

Only sliced fingertips are kissed
    and make the journey to your lips
Like inside-out glasses you sip
    our life's wine blooming like tulips

Now you see me with every eye
    with deer's, with owls', and with flies'
So I hear you in every sigh
    and taste your tears that never dry

There's no one like you in this world
    and yet the world seems full of you
I touch your hair in each vine curled
    I smell your neck in all perfume

Upon the pages of the sky,
    you write your verses in sunlight
and on the clouds like Sulayman
    I ride your breaths in sheer delight

On the blue page of the sky
    you write your book of clouds with sighs
So hot they turn the seas to flame
    burning lip-purple with your name

Until all is charred to black
    stars' ashes strewn across my back
Layla, what have you done to me?
    in your dark only can I see

And as the sparks sleep, dead and gone
    your black hair parts, breaking the dawn
The sun and moon, my pupils two
    whirl in eyes' dance, learning to read
    the music in our wave's bedsheets
Spinning out past the false and true
    —my dizzy art of loving you

On the pages of the clouds
    you paint lightning's calligraphy
And with your glance, without a sound
    you came and erased all of me
And snatched away my sight and mind
    again—your name in lightning signed

Your veil slipped from your face one time
and set the worlds ablaze with time
Sent them all spinning, love-sick, drunk
melting meaning to song and rhyme

Wherever I turn, there you are
with your beauty that's struck me blind
So I'm too dizzy to see you
nor can I reach you with my mind

I'll tie my body, like a rock
to this love note and toss it high
With desperate breaths and hopes your lips
will somehow find their way to mine

Next to you I'm less than nothing
I've got nothing except for you
You stole my soul, and my heart's wings
—nothing less than your shadow's truth

So nothingness is all I bring
to this table, my offering
Perhaps your love can still yet wring
more tears from my dry suffering

No more mornings, even evenings
past thought and beyond all feeling
past this, there's nothing but lies and
echoes of my only meaning

Oceans, mountains, deserts, ravines
clouds' shadows cross them all with ease
This dark can even outrun light
my listening far outstrips my sight

But in the twinkling of an eye
Sulayman snatched your throne and thighs
Your oceans of imagining
in his moist glance, have all run dry

The deserts of separation
all valleys of desperation
All vanish like mirages' lies
the twinkling of your heart's mirror sky

Your veil slipped from your face one time
    and set the worlds ablaze with time
So there's no time to fuss and cry
    come, quiet now, leave words behind

Cicadas

Turn my body into song
leave these words like cicada shells
Draw my soul through skies to you
trailing these clouds to tell my tale

Cicadas sang themselves away
and disappeared within your name
And with a glance, maybe a kiss
come help me now to do the same

A picture's worth a thousand words
    but poetry's contain vast herds
With centuries of movies full
    enfolded in each syllable

Because imagination's spring
    reflects all in its sweet running
It flows, carrying petals downstream
    as long as we breathe and birds sing

Close your mouth, open your eyes
    you'll see what these words can't describe
What hides behind the dark night sky
    the light that binds your soul to mine

Close your eyes, open your mouth
    I'll stop your talking with a kiss
And teach you to taste with your sight
    and see all with your dewy lips

Your beauty's just...

Too bright to see
    too hot to grasp
Blown away by
    your voice's blast
My soul's too weak
    for your perfume
But it tastes like
    the bright full moon
And given that
    all this is true
How could I hope
    to describe you?

The curve of your smile's the strength of my spine
    and this love in my heart's from the look in your eyes
And this passion's the scroll that is unfurled by time
    the words are all yours, but the handwriting's mine

Your dark glance shot into my heart
    a flute that bleeds out all my art
And like tapping a maple tree
    my sweetness flows out from pain's dart

My pen, don't weep so beautifully
    look how they love to wound soft trees
And burn their tears for their sweet scents
    see what your love has done to me

Is it better to live quietly
    or die as incense on your breeze?
Please don't despise these clouds, maybe
    soon they'll be all you've left of me

This love is writ in blood not ink
    its taste can't fit in what you think

I dipped my pen in my pupil
    to write my nights' pain without you
The tears of inky blood I cried
    all burned to black with desperate sighs
Like lightning trying to touch the moon
    are my words reaching out to you

My waves swelling to reach your sun
    and crashing in your reflection
My whole world's ended, dead and gone
    how is it that my life goes on?

Each breath I draw is like a blade
    each word, a heavy price that's paid
Strings bear the cost when they are played
    ears know not how the drumskin's flayed

Cut out my heart for its sweet juice
    hollow me out to make your flute
Fill me with blood blackened by sighs
    and for your flood I'll be a pipe

I'm helpless in this all, in truth
    it's your love you dipped me into
Until I crack and split in two
    I'll keep writing your songs for you

My heart's black speck's your pupil's eye
lined with ink-kohl from its black light
Your eye's moon rays dyed with ink's sight
night within day, day within night
Your glance is thus doubly eclipsed:
dark wines swirling 'twixt darker lips
Iris' center—a sea shoreless
lids' circumference—traceless phoenix

Like night's curls of separation
my tongue has grown dark and too long
From sipping, singing beauty's song
turned pen your dawn face draws upon

The inky cloak of love's mourning
dissolved in your sun-cheeked morning

My heart's black hole's holding inside
all eyes reveal, all that ears hide
The back and forth of lightning strikes
your two brows, the two bows in flight
Like crescents 'cross the desert night
like verses 'cross the page's blight
Like two lips' kissed and holding tight
night's *qadr, mi'raj* of endless light

From the mighty tree of life,
I made a book of love
Written with eyelashes' pens,
ink tears and bound in blood

My hands sticky from knowing sap
juice running down my chin
My body's stuck to these pages
soul bound to what's within

These breaths burnished to shining mirrors
flowing, reflecting sky
Whose inky night gleams with bright stars
light streams that won't run dry

My soul unfurls out from my lips
in smoke curls like your hair
Hold me under your dark nightgown
to perfume all that's there

Love's lightning turned my tree of life
into a burning bush
My pens bore flaming fruit whose seeds'
hot ash made sky's ink blush

When beauty's sun, like Sulayman
rides on the breeze at dawn
Then kiss your words and life goodbye
love comes and they're all gone

خمريّات

Wine Odes

Variation on Hafez's Ghazal #1

Hey son, pour me another one
for love is sweet, and my life's done

Fill up a cup with wine's warm light
my heart feels like it weighs a ton

Love starts out like a melody
but ends in tears, dry, without sound

How can kids lying on the beach
know what it's like for we who've drowned?

How can those who've yet to begin
know what it's like to face your end?

To sleep upon a bed of waves
beneath a sheet woven of wind

In love, there's nothing to hold on
to, save love's self—no star, no friend

So when you catch a whiff of love
or your heart beats from its far drum

Just drop the world, leave it behind
forget yourself and come

This life's too hard to live sober
    so drink and try to die a drunk
For heaven's but a hangover
    for those who drink from your mouth's cup

And when I miss your lips I mix
    love's memories with words in verse
To warm my soul with little sips
    and cool the sharp pain of my thirst

So pour love's lightning in my heart
    and grind my bones to gleaming sparks
All dancing like stars on the tides
    my life's shores end where your love starts

If you spent your life for a drop
    that's cheap—it won't have been in waste
And all your life has been for naught
    if you die now without a taste

So all I have's a burning heart
    fed by tears flowing like the rain
Lips scalded by love's tongues of flame
    can never taste death's bitter pain

After one taste of your lips, all else has lost its taste
    so kiss me soon or kill me now or my life's gone to waste

The sharp lines of my mind now cling to your curves for dear life
    my thoughts are dancing, swinging like the beads around your waist

Time seems to bend in your black eyes, like curls around your face
    eternity's a blink compared to what you make me wait

I want to crawl under the earth, I want to fly beyond the skies
    I'll drag my soul through any hole, so long as it ends by your side

I drank a drink of love that drank me too
a bottomless bottle shaped much like you

When I was drunk, my hands around its waist
it seemed where'er I spun, I saw your face

Or maybe in wine, you were seeing mine?
Time consumes all, but your mouth snacks on Time

And like the sun approaching nightfall's lips
mine burned purple with promise of a kiss

When to the glass's lip your own came near
my blood turned ink and stained the water clear

My intention's in tension with your lips
—don't spit me out like all of those date pits

As the bartender said, taking my keys,
"Life's rough, stay loose and never lock your knees

And if you sin, then sin with a princess
and if you drink, make it the best vintage

True, we all trade our life and mind for wine
at least make it *Alast*'s, which outlasts time

Don't sell your tear-pearled heart-gem so cheaply
your intellect's worth this wine-kissed ruby

Don't wait too long before making the trade
this soul, that wine turn vinegar with age."

So I keep my lips moist, sipping your name
and if one day, you should visit my grave

Then from my veins, grape vines and violets
will grow, fragrant like wine, just like your lips

You're but a cork sealing you from yourself
pop it off and drink deep to your own health

Your mouth's Sulayman's seal, a rose corkscrew
that frees spirits, so winds get drunk on you

This vast vat that from you to you I pour
    from my sky to my sea's no shore nor floor

I drank a drink of love that drank me too
    as love's flames consumed me, I drowned in you

If you see cup and wine as two, you haven't drunk enough
in this tavern, we drink love's molten glass, served by the cup

And when the sparkling wine is swirled and left still to breathe well
that's just the glass-blower whispering his secret sculpting spells

Not only does this wine redden cups' sweet cheeks and their lips
its pouring gives them lovely shapes and their bright translucence

The heavens are but spinning glasses cast from frozen wine
how strange that they all seem to fit within this cup of mine

Inside my glass, last night, I saw your face, mingling with mine
in drunken clarity, I sipped myself in your outline

The fine lines of your lips are just the rippling of this wine
and so we drink and kiss 'till I can't tell what's yours from mine

Last night, I got so drunk I sold my soul for cups of wine
I'm back to see what I can get for my body this time

My heart's the secret flask of that most thirsty of madmen
who drained the wine, drank the dry glass, then downed the whole tavern

Bilqis thought our way water, but soon learned this glass held wine
Sulayman's tricked many spirits into these bottles of rhymes

Though everyone loves wine's bouquet, who likes the drunkard's belch?
Be quiet, hold your drink, and keep its secrets to yourself.

غزلیات

Ghazals

How could you leave me all alone?
    Even Adam didn't fall alone

We're all walking each other home
    But we must enter all alone

Though we're one vast and cloudy choir
    We all answer the call alone

And like stars in the morning dawn
    We fade within your pall alone

Before your beauty's blinding sun
    Only mad love stands tall alone

Though we're from one soul, ranged in ranks
    We all must breathe and bawl alone

You said you're closer than my soul
    How can I walk this hall alone?

Remember now, these words are true:
    You'll never run, walk, crawl alone

Feel, I'm the beat in your heart when
    You're up against the wall alone

You're my dream, I see through your eyes
    Only I wake up all alone

So Sulayman with all his hosts
    Bows before you who's All, Alone

Your light made me shade, small, alone
    Without shadow, you're all alone

Time's just shadows' race after you
there's no before or after you

I sprinkled tears on your footprints
so their dust won't run after you

My eyes, clouded by grief and sighs,
cried rivers running after you

Your voice breathed life into my clay
these sad songs copy after you

I close my eyes just to see yours
in black mirrors pointing after you

I close my lips just to kiss yours
'cause there's no sweetness after you

My heart broke, but love's blaze burns on
boat's wrecked, the sea storms after you

Where did you hide? And where've I gone?
I know there's no me after you

Last night, stumbling to my heart's room
I held the door, said, "after you"

You plucked all the fruits from both worlds
so hungry, I came after you

You glanced and made the atoms dance
all lovelorn, chasing after you

The sun and moon in their orbits,
unfixed, all stars run after you

Please look at me, have some pity
without me, who'll pine after you?

You seem always before my eyes
—I can't seem to look after you

I rehearsed what to say to you
on what I went through after you

You came, my tongue clove to the roof
there's no more talking after you

The wealth of Sulayman and his
    wisdom are just drafts after you

Your love's my life, and mine's its end
    there's no before or after you

Love's no escape nor a way in
    there's no before nor after you

Today, I've lost another friend, though death is not the end
    tonight, millions more souls ascend, though death is not the end

This life's a crumbling cliff's edge, weeping earth endlessly
    the clouds cry, I lose you again, though death is not the end

What have you found here to hold on to, when all seems condemned
    where we all lose all, all is loss, though death is not the end

Last night I heard a gazelle cry, against extinction's blaze
    it poured out groans, like sea waves' foam, though death is not the end

See how high have the towers grown, like gleaming glass gravestones
    they've buried all that can't be owned, though death is not the end

Some days I wish death would bring an end to its suffering
    but even for itself I know, no, death is not the end

I've been missing you so long, longing itself grew tired of us
    from light to ash, rivers to snow, know death is not the end

And like a flock of butterflies, migrating the seasons
    we wander in and out of time, so death is not the end

Falling through our hands like rain, time's precious pearls, too rare to spend
    on anything but making love, though death is not the end

Though death is not the end, when will our separations cease?
    I'm getting sick of being told that death is not the end

Only your mouth can stop my cries and seal this sad lament
    these words echo 'twixt ribs and stars, for death is not their end

That mighty seal of Sulayman, commanding all the jinn's
    the imprint of your angel kiss, for which death is no end

Wake up my love and give me life with kisses without end
    lie down and sleep with me again, so death won't be the end

If everything's so wrong, how could you ever be right here?
    and if you won't come down, please, at least don't leave me right here

For years I've searched night skies for answers to life's mysteries
    until the sunrise of your mouth's rose bloomed, told me, "Right here."

That sigh that tousled inky locks and set free your perfume
    collapsed the walls of my small room and buried me right here

I've battled my share of demons and times as hard as steel
    who knew that lips soft as petals could cut through me right here

Why put your joy on layaway? The rates are bad, I hear
    when there's so much fun to be had with you and me right here?

The spring of life's so far away, but you're closer than near
    for your whispers in my ear, I'd give all of me right here

There's nothing left for me but you, I got lost in your eyes
    where all the smart men charged ahead, you told me, "Turn right here"

This world is killing all my friends, outside and inside too
    death may not be the end, but grief's endless, hold me right here

This life's a vast desert mirage that drinks all efforts dry
    where's the escape from this fake sky? You said to me, "Right here"

'Cause right now, I just want to rest with you beneath a tree
    the world's ablaze and so's my heart as you can see right here

If all the trees became my pens, my ink, the seven seas
    I couldn't hope to write your beauty that I see right here

I used to think that life is but two days, one in, one out
    but now I know they're just the two lips of your mouth right here

I'm but a cloud before your sun, I make its beams appear
    your naked truth comes out only when there's no me right here

Where is the realm of Sulayman that surpassed all the rest?
    you pulled my head down to your breast, whispered to me "right here"

Where is that paradise of love that we all miss and fear?
    your hands held my heart in their grasp and it cried, "Me! Right here!"

What lies beyond the heavens? Behind all we think or hear?
    "Well, out past all these lies," you laughed, "there's only me, right here."

With your excess of beauty, you should give some charity
    for God's sake, it's easy, you'll always find poor me right here

When I could, I knew not; when I knew, I could not
though sun's light sees all sights, its own view, eyes could not

Though I've spent lifetimes in search of your beauty's mouth
when I had a chance to see it through, I could not

Holding my breath for years, waiting to talk to you
when I tried to confess the whole truth, I could not

Though beauty is but one, lovers' ways are diverse
from rose hips, I refrain, from yours too, I could not

From Azal, we cocooned ourselves under time's roof
but when off to Abad, they all flew, I could not

Though I spent all my life building towers of proofs
when I tried to find love's alleys' clues, I could not

Wandr'ing through valleys once I found myself within
Tuwa, but take off my two worn shoes, I could not

Your black hair is so long, and my life's been cut short
but express the small bits that I knew, I could not

I see all foundations save love's are deeply flawed
in my heart's flawless mirror, see but you, I could not

Solid as shifting clouds, stable as crashing waves
did you find any here that stay true? I could not

You love's blaze burned my brain, turned my soul to blue flame
though Hell's flames grew and grew, give up you, I could not

Like a flute, I only speak when you blow through me
I threw not, when I threw, it was you, I could not

When upon the dead earth, your shade falls, dunes all bloom
but up from my dry grave, poems grew, I could not

Like angels, your poets hymn your praise, constantly
how could I hope to that song outdo, I could not

"Don't despair of my mercy for you," came a thought
if you wish, Love will find a way through, I could not

With your love, we would see others do what you do
the moon and my heart split into two, I could not

What is impossible next to what ought to be?
    even water, with your magic touch, I could knot

With my tears, on the lake, I trace your face's lines
    but erase with my sighs, what eyes drew, I could not

When I wake beside you, all dreams and songs come true
    with you, I see all truth, without you, I could not

I am trapped in your mirror, waiting all night for you
    but regard my reflection anew, I could not

Champagne for your sham friends, real pain for your real friends
    in the end, damn the cost, betray you, I could not

Humming like bees seeking meaning between the straw
    gather all beauty that your hands strew, I could not

I've had so many suitors who've sought my rough hand
    though they all asked me to follow through, I could not

All I have is on loan to one day be repaid
    though my debts all were long overdue, I could not

Drunk on this, or on that, sober life is too hard
    I'm dead drunk, though I've tried to come to, I could not

Whisp'ring here, singing there, beauty's scent's everywhere
    what could keep love's secret? I've tried to, I could not

Combing your kinky hair's knots and twists I have come
    all undone, claiming name or virtue, I could not

All colors spring from sun's light broke in airy dew
    when sun glanced down on blue sea, its hue, I could not

Show me your face one time, take me out of my mind
    I'm your veil, who could lift it but you, I could not

If I had Sulayman's wisdom I wouldn't do
    half of what your love has put me through, I could not

Who knows what you could do, once I knew I could not
    your sun rose, our shadows all withdrew, I could not

I fall fast, deep asleep my dreams rise to her lips
    she coughs and feels my soul as it flies to her lips

I send my tears to you on my sighs like sea breeze
    salty-sweet, let my hopes and prayers rise to her lips

Before dawn, my tongue was set loose by her love's wine
    my heart's full, red moon breaks, splits, divides to her lips

Oh my heart, try to wait patiently loving her
    only when meat's roasted can it rise to her lips

Like a chameleon I've tried to hide my love
    but my sighs make rainbows, who could lie to her lips?

My heart's so full of her that she flows down my cheeks
    I'll sneak into her heart, otherwise, through her lips

If my own river can't find the ocean so what?
    as long as her love drips from my eyes to her lips

At the end of the day, I fall into her lips
    Sulayman's birds and words all fly wise through her lips

Here am I counting stars in your night-shining hair
    my moon heart counts its scars in your hands over there

Where did you go my love that no one found you there?
    "True, One hides in herself, and I wear every where"

There you go once again—my soul's dust in your wake
    "I'll be back soon to take your body over there"

Here I am, but my mind and the world now have fled
    all I've left is my passion for you over here

"There, don't leave love behind, it has always been mine
    come now, there's nothing for you, my dear, over there"

What I sought in my heart's embers blown to bright coals
    by your breath, I found in your eyes' kohl-covered lairs

Your beauty's violence shattered my bright silence
    my soul tossed like a scarf cov'ring your hair for prayer

Lightning falling like rain from your face on my tongue
    burnished breaths climb to you, poems hover in air

Your love came like a flood, washed my knowledge away
    all I now can recall: "Lips and hearts come in pairs"

I reached out for your hand, found it inside my sleeve
    how are you everywhere, and yet not over there?

When the earth is shaken and the clouds burst in flame
    my body's in your Name, and my soul in your stare

Overcome by the sight of you standing alone
    if there's only you, how can I come over there?

Where can I stand a chance to get a glimpse of You?
    the ground went up in smoke when your lovers got there

Now I float like a cloud in your night, without care
    just a lock of your hair, neither here, nor out there

Hold your breath, Sulayman's been crowned King of the air
    go whistle your sad songs to someone over there

Your smile flashed and took my soul back home
    your pupil is my black stone and black home

Your lightning glances burned my clay to glass
    your curls' black mirrors call, beckon me back home

Your eyelashes' rakes combed over the town
    and harvested hearts from poor, ransacked homes

Fate's missiles blew holes in mind's azure dome
    no mansion's as wide as my lilac's home

Thorns' curse as dear as petal's kiss to me
    fire's treasure in a maniac's home

One who's seen you won't ever see sleep's rest
    your scent makes mansions of our horseback homes

My body in ruins, soul on its last legs
    I break out, you break into this cracked home

The fire is lit, bed's with roses strewn
    the water is warm, so hurry back home

My eye is your home, my heart is your world
    though you can't leave one, join both, come back home

The builders and divers of Solomon
    diverse loves, become one in you, back home

The stars have not forgotten us
    we've drowned them in streetlights

The paths have not darkened, they need
    sparks that your swift feet light

My soul's cold sorrows all thawed in
    your glances like heat lights

Your love has soaked me to the bone
    my tears glow, I bleed light

I take my tea, just like my life
    like your kisses, sweet, light

Your beauty broke all laws, just like
    Sulayman unseats light

Now we've forgotten all the stars
    drowned, drunk in your sweet light

Lions and volcanoes roar
because they're missing you

My heart's been burnt down to its core
because it's missing you

The earth split and the heavens tore
because they're missing you

The full moon became my soul's door
because it's missing you

Pronouns are three, the seasons' four
because they're missing you

You're my five senses and sickness
because I'm missing you

My soul holds what your sweet lips pour
because it's missing you

My heart's sore but cries out for more
because it's missing you

And with my soul, I sweep your floor
because I'm missing you

Because they're missing you, my veins
became richer than Sulayman

And just because it's missing you
my hand glows brighter than the sun

Because it's kissing you, my heart
broken in two, has become one

What's all this murmuring?
    these voices that cried out?
The hubbub of lovers'
    bubbles turned inside-out

From the wine floating up
    or the gasps you sighed out
From your dark, love-stained lips,
    pleasure's secret hide-out

Now I've come to that spring
    where the poems slide out:
Teary eyes that have seen
    your mouth bloom in sly pout

Where's all that music gone?
    has sun's fire died out?
My heart dragged out to sea
    when your moon's tide is out

So my tongue is tied up
    and my mouth is dried out
By bright beauty's desert
    when love's hot wind rides out

Bubbles enter heaven
    heads popped, all pride blown out
Smoke's sad candle's secret
    laughing fire pried out

Your kiss eclipsed my mind
    stealing off with my doubt
But what if, I wonder
    something more we tried out?

Now, this life's but a dream
    and the next's a mirage
That we run to thirsty
    finding now naught but God

Sulayman had a ring
    on which your name's engraved
and you'll find the same thing
    on my heart, in my grave

What's all this murmuring,
    echoes in my heart's cave?
Sun's setting of the stars
    the rain kissing the waves

Your beauty makes the atoms dance
    that's the delight of all the worlds
And turns us into longing flames
    that's just the plight of all the worlds

Your hair falls like black lightning strikes
    your eyes sparkle with all the stars,
With all the dark mystery and art,
    of all the nights of all the worlds

What strange drinks does your rose mouth mix
    and pouring love, your sweet lips make
Me stumble drunk, without a care
    and bear the spite of all the worlds

And even when I can't see it
    your face shines out from everywhere
Just like the sun hid in clouds' veils
    your smile's the light of all the worlds

The whole world's your shadow's shadow
    where his glance falls, there we all go
Reflections in your mirror thirst for
    your eyes, the sight of all the worlds

And if your shade should fall on me
    if I should climb into your eyes
A dream, I would come true as you
    make right the slights of all the worlds

Your beauty sets our souls aloft
    and binds us to your loveliness
Set free, tossed in your tangled locks
    your hair makes kites of all the worlds

Each part of me's filled with passion
    for all of you, who are my all
Apart from you, who could we call,
    what could we write of all the worlds?

Sulayman had at his command
    all of the might of all the worlds
—Less than an eyelash on your cheek
    your sigh makes light of all the worlds

When all is lost, then all is won
    but it's much easier said than done
And when all has been said and done
    it's so much easier said when done

But it's so difficult to say
    just how your love has struck me dumb
Perhaps easier done than said
    or not easier said than done

For I'm your sacrifice today
    my poor heart crushed to little crumbs
Please finish what you start, I pray—
    —bled out, liver charred, well and done

Although I've tripped, cut myself on
    shards gleaming with your reflection
Make this last step I stumble on
    be your bed, where I lie undone

My soul's worn-out and weighs a ton
    my flesh is wrecked like chewed-up gum
Cheeks, cracked deserts where rivers run
    —my burning tears, sun-red and dun

Your sight brings my heart back to life
    your breath makes my body stand tall
Your lips make me to understand
    and overcome sweet abandon

Sulayman stole Queen Sheba's throne
    like my heart, easier done than said
Crossing his vast desert of mirrors
    is much easier dead than done

I've lost all but these songs for you
    the echoes of my heart, long gone
I'll follow these breaths back to you
    'cause it's much easier said and done

Every thing was al-
right, but then you left
Even the sun seemed
all wrong when you left

You didn't put two
hearts into my chest
But broke it into
pieces when you left

You told me to count
kisses on my neck
Before I made it
up to ten, you left

Remember when you
split moons with a smile?
You shattered the world
to bits when you left

I heard your sweet voice
coming from the waves
Before I could pick
up a pen, you left

I saw your beauty
shining through the clouds
But then I blinked rain
and again, you left

I went off to pray
and caught your scent there
But before we all
said, "Amen," you left

I even taste you
inside my hot tears
My eyes burning like
the cayenne you left

If only you had
left me completely
Love wouldn't drag me
around when you left

My life, you left me
  a body sans soul
Tossed on the mountain
  of dead men you left

Now I'm just a ghoul,
  soul without body,
Doomed to haunt circling
  'round the den you left

See what you've become
  a crescent fading
Before winking stars
  of women you left

Listen, Sulayman
  if you want her back
Put your ring back on
  look again, who left?

But after the dawn
  dissolves all this smoke
There's only, ever,
  always been you left

With you, I'm nothing
    without you, nothing

There's nothing that I
    could say on nothing

What could you tell me
    when I am no thing?

Every thing is yours
    can I bring nothing?

Dawn breaks, shadows live
    what's added? Nothing

Sun shines, and I die
    who misses nothing?

Night falls, you know what
    my eyes see? Nothing

But something's still wrong,
    bothering my nothing

What's all this talking?
    you're all, I'm nothing

I keep noticing
    this, so who's nothing?

If you're all seeing
    then who sees nothing?

Nothing escapes you,
    but I'm bound to you
If I were nothing
    wouldn't I slip through?

For God's sake hold your tongue and let me love, no, let it go
    or hold my pen 'til language love outgrows, so let it go

My body's a snowflake wat'ring a garden of bright flames
    my soul's a fly bewitched by your bright cheek's glow, let it go

The treasures from those glances that I stole so long ago
    with ten lives, I could not pay back what I owe, let it go

My heart's an hourglass half-filled with blood and half with tears
    your beauty and love spinning it make life flow, let it go

These beads of sweat and prayer between my hands are all seeking
    those beads around your waist, switching to and fro, let it go

Your beauty took my sense hostage and held my body so,
    I've got nothing left to pay their ransom, so let it go

My poetry, like dove's cooing, is all lovely, 'til when
    love comes and make me choke it down like old crow, let it go

You shoot those deadly glances carelessly, aim at my heart
    my soul's drawn tighter than the string on your bow, let it go

Your beauty's persuasion's sharper than proofs, stronger than bombs
    love's wind will bear my ashes falling like snow, let it go

I'm dancing, weeping, smiling, burning in your light's shadows
    I'm just a candle waiting for your lips' blow, let it go

"I've given up all joys for you, I'm waning like the moon."
    She said, "Your fasting's going way too slow though, let it go."

"I'll go on quests and win knowledge, and fame, and gold for you."
    She said, "My mouth's the end of every rainbow, let it go."

I worked out, got dressed up, washed clean my soul for you, but then
    your lightning strike consumed me head to toe, so let it go

"I got caught in your undertow, love dragged me out to sea."
    —"Come willingly next time, or I'll just, you know, let it go."

My mama said to never throw a stone and hide my hand
    but worlds are hidden within me when you throw, let it go

My heart’s narcissus spot is your love’s brand and eye’s pupil
I know my eyes’ brightness is just your shadow, let it go

I said, “Sulayman’s fine kingdom of songs now lies in ruins...”
She said, “Over each soul a Hafez flies, so let it go.”

Truth is, for me, hell, with you'd be heaven
    Lying in your arms, this world beats heaven

Love's shoreless ocean's my only haven
    A port in grief's storm's how we see heaven

If your scent's shadow fell on the garden
    In search of your face, we'd all flee heaven

And if your crescent smiles down on me then
    My bent spine would bear earth and the heavens

Passion's monsoon falls, and steamy sighs rise
    Clouds' tears douse the flames setting free heaven

Don't turn me away, my love keeps you warm
    Without thorns, what would your rose be? Heaven?

If tiny ants could talk to Sulayman
    My small love waits on your beauty's heaven

Heaven is a ring tossed in love's desert
    And Sulayman's is my heart's key, heaven

All of the worlds swirl into my pupil
    My heart's love's black hole, gravity's heaven

The paradises opened wide at dawn
    —I rolled over, next time, maybe heaven

Each breath and every step I take
    —a new heartbreak, after heartbreak

How many times can you split souls
    until the atoms of hearts break?

This wound's a toungeless mouth that aches,
    longs for lips' wine to cure heartbreak

My life's a blister on love's feet
    whose dance crushes our hearts like grapes

She kicks up ruby dust's dawnbreak
    her glance pops heavens, our hearts break

Under imagination's rain
    all colors, all thoughts, all hearts break

Like Musa's staff, and 'Isa's sighs
    Sulayman's feats rise from heartbreak

Throw down your pen, watch it take flight
    ink's love makes paper's pure heart break

Please, no more pastors, shaykhs, oh no
    just take me to babalawo

The oracle of the sincere,
    all others are voices of woe

Great shows of piety outside
    but what they do inside...Ah! Whoa!

Sermons sprayed like a fire hose,
    I'd prefer screeching hoot owls

With shaking jowls, and lech'rous growls
    they've shocked even all that is foul

Flames' tongues of love tell hearts' secrets
    dried dung's smoke's different from aloes'

To tell this tale, plain speech won't do
    we'll need some drums, and long flute's howls

Though secrets can be spilt I know
    Sulayman's mystery's mute, awo

This heart's a coal that pulses with each sweet gust of your breath
hidden beneath this body of ash dancing on your breath

The tears are falling like stars, making a new Milky Way
across my soul's dark night lit by the moonlight of your breath

Roses' petals, nightingales' wings are united at last
when burnt to ashes by sighs like solar flares of your breath

My head fell ashen with grief from failing you in this love
my limbs condemn me, reach for mercy perfumed by your breath

The lightning flashed and burned life's flowing sands into bright glass
which thunder's gasp polished so it could hold onto your breath

The pens of fate ran dry, so they dipped their beaks in my blood
and scratched my life out upon the sheer pages of your breath

Leave it behind, don't chase shadows as the sky's ripening
here comes the sun, what can candles find but death on your breath?

Don't think you're wise if you haven't chased mirages like me
you haven't tasted that thirst for her beauty on your breath

Hidden in every sight and revealed in every hiding
this robe of words and vast worlds came all undone on your breath

Trampled and ground to bits by the stallions of your beauty
my crushed clay rose as dust coming back to life on your breath

I whispered your name to winds to bear my secret away
last night, they all fell in love, today they tell on your breath

So you wear my heart like wind wears leaves, like song wears a voice
and like your will wears a choice, we're all floating on your breath

So like the clouds, my chest's glowing from the gleams of your face
and my pen's flute is crying ghazals from gusts of your breath

Unless your pen's been chewed in the sweetness of my dawn mouth
who'd want a whiff of that inky bouquet's stain on your breath?

The full moon of your shadow tugs at my ocean of grief
your sun face stirs up delight, eyes' sails fly out on your breath

Though Sulayman conquered all the winds, your sigh conquered me
you knocked the wind out of me, blow me away on your breath

Your eyes sing "come here," your mouth says, "get lost"
my hands in your curls, hearts in lips get lost

My cheeks are criss-crossed by footprints of tears
in your flawless face, all traces get lost

My sins have all found their cause in your mouth
in your dazzling face, perfection gets lost

Your glance skewered my heart, stuck me to now's spot
I'm time's shaft's shadow, I cannot get lost

There's hundreds of hearts strung on your tasbih
string breaks and the beads, bewildered, get lost

The thousands of souls hung round your slim neck
reflect your smile and lightning gets lost

Sighs' clouds swallow tears and scatter rainbows
rain's rhythm inside thunder's sobs gets lost

This wine stumbles drunk and gambles my blood
your love covers all bets and my debts' loss

Khayal's sweet song bonds senses into worlds
you kiss me and all of my dreams get lost

You only seek what is not in your hands
you say "silence" and its meaning gets lost

Why polish when dust is just tiny mirrors?
vast heavens in your pupils' dots get lost

I found all colors, scents, songs in your eyes
all of the worlds in your tears' pearls get lost

Bilqis, Sulayman, dance on the water
mirrors meet face to face and vision gets lost

With all these black mirrors, it's hard to get lost?
looking in your eyes, my home, I get lost

We feast all day and drink all night
because it's Ramadan
We dance and sing our heart's delight
because it's Ramadan
Our souls unbound, we fly like planes
because it's Ramadan
Cops get caught in our cast-off chains
because it's Ramadan
So we climb roofs and go insane
because it's Ramadan
The haters are too tired to hate
because it's Ramadan
Sorrows become as sweet as dates
because it's Ramadan
Your beauty blooms like the full moon
because it's Ramadan
My love burns like the sun at noon
because it's Ramadan
We drink lightning and eat thunder
because it's Ramadan
Our eyes wide with sleepless wonder
because it's Ramadan
On your light, feast, in my dark, fast,
because it's Ramadan
Time moves so slow, it's turning back,
because it's Ramadan
I give up all my loves but You,
because it's Ramadan
My love, don't give up on me too,
because it's Ramadan
Your kisses are my main dishes
because it's Ramadan
Your glance is what water for fish is
because it's Ramadan

Because it's Ramadan, bring me a cup of that strong drink
That makes, not breaks the lovers' fast and clears mosques with a wink
I break my fast with air when I lift my mouth from the cup
Your lips are just too fine for God to ask me to give up

Ah Love, let down your hair, relax, because it's Ramadan
Let's go outside and kiss 'til dawn while the rain recites Qur'an

Come let's scatter tears of pearls like the moon
in mem'ry of that face scarred like the moon

In spring's first month of the last rose's bloom
the petals fall dark and new like the moon

You're gone but the whole world's shot through with you
my heart, blood-filled, broke in two like the moon

From East to the West the legions of doom
have shadowed all save those true like the moon

The thousands of blows from thousands of foes
feel light when your smile's in view like the moon

Your night's million hairs your stare's bright lashes
beat back black batons withdrew like the moon

This one drinks wine, but that one drinks blood, so
who's more ashamed be- fore you, like the moon?

Her hair's henna-dyed and his beard, with blood
which is dusk, which, dawn? which bruised like the moon?

Your dark locks' the key to dawn's victory
your breeze's scent came: hope grew like the moon

Pride's cancer inside, the white wolves outside
drown in wine's tides, be renewed like the moon

If dark clouds should come to smother your tongue
be quiet, appear in dew, like the moon

How can those heart-thieves be so heartless too?
look what they make lovers go through, like the moon

The pious just love their bloated mirror's pride
their eyes clouded and askew like the moon

The lovers just love you and all you've dyed
in water they all see you like the moon

The leprous hearts claim to speak in His Name
the nameless reflect what's true like the moon

Your work is to shine, to wonder is mine
and then disappear in blue like the moon

The worship of po- -wer's such bloody work
slaught'ring the lambs for their hue, like the moon

My tears stoked heart's flames and like the leaves' fire
beneath autumn rains they grew like the moon

If they want to spill our blood out tonight
leap up and let them pursue like the moon

The soldiers of sep- -aration's night cut
joy short but its light regrew like the moon

The waves of darkness the mountains of clouds
your locks' perfume can undo like the moon

Though they try to trap you in their box, your
beauty escapes ca- -mera's view like the moon

These days are dark dreams nights, tears' clouds of sighs—
both fog that your face shines through like the moon

With my tears your love has made its own mirror
on each breath, like tides you drew like the moon

Since your reflection fell into its glass
my heart has a new worldview, like the moon

This night seems long but dawn's fire's in view
the days of this life —so few like the moon's

I've seen such evil my heart's fallen dark
in part, but the whole's in view like the moon

The sun blushes from your cheeks' rose garden
so I'm pining for you too, like the moon

How did Sulayman's wisdom fill the world?
he told not all his heart knew like the moon

Let's climb on heaven and make a new sky
in footprints of those who flew like the moon

Come let's scatter tears like stars in dark wine
drunk, swirling its cup 'round you like the moon

مرثیات

Elegies

An Elegy for George Floyd[1]

Did lightning just flash from the far northern plains?
 Or is it thunder crying out with their names?
Is it from recalling our beloved slain
 that tears mix with blood in the hot, heavy rain?
Or has the tear gas on the smoked southern breeze
 brought news of strange fruit, from new, mace-perfumed trees?
Is that dawn in the West? Or the midnight firelight?
 Has the sun finally set on this nightmarish life?

Red sky at morning, old soldiers take warning
 You strike a rock, and the earth quakes in mourning

The long night withheld its sweet sleep from me
 Like grains in my eyes are the bitter killings
His murder made ev'n the driest eyes weep,
 the heartless of this age ripe with mis'ry

Our tears fell like rain, as vast as the seas
 but vanish in their desert's sympathy
How then to write, for George, elegy?
 my only ink's tears, my paper's burning
My grief has made me a pillar of salt
 the water's run out, but the sobs will not halt
On God, I'll mourn you as long as there's talking
 as long as the flesh on my bones moves with longing

How can I praise you, when we cannot breathe?
 When there are no more words, what words do we need?
Bring music, light fires, let them see us bleed
 What can we say now, except, "now you fly free."

He cried for his dead, 'cause the living were deaf
 But where were you, God, at his hard, last breath?
—We are closer to him, but you do not see
 I was sick, you ain't visit; hungry, nothing to eat

1. This poem first appeared on the *Sapelo Square* website: https://sapelosquare.com/2020/06/10/an-elegy-for-george-floyd/, republished here with the permission of *Sapelo Square*.

And dying, you choked me, 'till I couldn't breathe—
    But what of the murderous devil, his knee?
—take refuge from such dark shadows in Me—

God, your lovers are fine but your fan club's a mess
    and I'm honestly not too sure 'bout the rest
the earth's choked with so much injustice and greed
    Where is there left any humanity?
What shrouds can we stitch with shreds of decency?
    Is it only in death that we can be free?

There's none like him in life, and there never will be
    but in death, he joins a vast company:
Ahmaud, Breonna, Trayvon, and Sandra
    Philando and Alton, Atatiana
Amadou, 'Umar, Funmi, Adama
    Biko, Cabral, Emmett, Lumuumba
Breffu, Boukman, Makandal, Dandará
    Tamir, Tony, David, Walter, Mujinga
Takyi and Jati, Bouna, Eliza
    Michael and Eric, our mothers and fathers
Huey and Medgar, and Malcolm and Martin
    Millions more—names lost—but they, not forgotten

For you, I will weep as long as doves cry
    As long as the stars and the moon in the sky
brighten the way of a kind passer-by
    As long as the truth stands out from the lies
As long as there's water and light in the eyes
    and warmth in a hug, soft strength our thighs

I'll never make peace with your enemies
    There's no truce for light with shadows of fleas
We fight and we struggle, how? By any means.
    'til the sun's burned to ashes, all cold and unseen
    'til we reach that home where life's just a dream

What'd we do to you, Death, that you do us like this?
    I know life's unfair, but where's your justice?

My heart's well of tears is rising higher
    they toss bodies in, our souls catch fire

They trample and curse, spit, shit all on ours
    and just like the earth, we keep feeding them flowers
It seems some evils even time can't devour
    because they refuse to repent 'till the Hour

Time's gnawed at this wound, and bit me and cut
    it's about damn time, even Hell says "enough!"

No doubt, we'll beat those who've forgotten defeat
    their bloody idylls are perched on clay feet
Their idols all stained by the lives of the meek
    as they sacrifice us for their cannibal feasts

Their laws and their order are causes of murder
    the jaws of their jails filled with dreamers deferred

The Big House is built on our ancestor's bones
    bricks baked with their blood, sweat mortars each stone
What ghouls could ever call such places home?
    Only the most hungry, amnesiac ghosts

But with all of these bodies in the wall
    this house built on crimes is bound to soon fall
Like 'Ad and Thamud, like Rome, Babylon
    this piled-up dust will be scattered and gone

God bless all those brave and desperate souls
    thrown out in the fields, shivering in the cold
Nothing left to lose, no more fucks to give
    they give all the fire to stand up and live

The comfortable kneel and pray for taut peace
    but real ones are out here stirring up a breeze

I envy the birds, I envy the trees
    they've never seen such from their own species
Our hearts are broken, now smash theirs, diseased
    return them to form, or destroy the donkeys!

Come down now Moses! Your people are dying!
    Ditch the palace, come run with the lions
There's no time to wait, no place for hiding
    Kick off your shoes and come take us flying

Part the waters, make Sinai's climb
    Bring down the light and the fire this time

You were sent as a mercy to the Red and the Black
    Now our black blood runs red from the stripes on our backs
from the blows of the Pharoah's warlocks and their staffs
    Deaf, dumb, and blind, will they never go back?
Intercede now and heal us, they're on the attack
    Have we not always sheltered the people of Haqq?

They lie on our skins, dance and feast on our pain
    And then pretend to care, liars without shame
Their faces like death, armored, masked in hate
    The legion Christ cast into pigs now renamed

God give us the strength, and please keep us sane
    Please grant us justice, and keep us humane
From Oakland to Addis, London to Brisbane
    We ask by our best, your Mightiest Name
Have mercy upon all of our friends slain
    by poverty, hate, by illness and Cain
they're not dead, but living, in skies and our veins
    Bless all our mothers, our sisters in pain
Bless our fathers and our brothers in chains
    Bless all those who stand with us not for fame
    And grant us a good end, free of any shame

But now we'll still shout and still dance and still sing
    the desperate joy of the last human beings

Did lightning just flash from the far northern plains?
    Or is its thunder crying out in our pain?

Jerusalem

I saw thousands of prayers rise up like flares
    nightly, o'er an iron dome
Then dozens of souls, the young and the old
    dispatched by hearts colder than stone
The Prophets gathered on mount and valley
    in spirit and deep in the bones
As Pharaohs parade in Moses' clothes,
    new Edomites tear down old homes

The spirit of God moves over the gas
    that's made tears flow into salt seas
The Temple Mount groans, Aqsa's boulders moan
    and even the olive trees weep
How can we sing the old songs of joy
    in lands without justice or peace?

Above the flood, doves' cries echo in deeps
    at Hope and Love bound and slaughtered like sheep
And butchered, or shot in bed while asleep
    across the land, blood's spilled, plague's rot still creeps

Those scarred outside stand, struggle, starve, and watch
    as those scarred inside sit and feast
The rockets' red glare, the hate in the air
    puts to shame all the wild beasts

They take what they want without any right
    because they are wrong, because they are white
Because they've been wronged, they think that it's might
    that turns all the wrongs left behind into right

How could the ladder dreamed by Israel
    make of the land of the Isra', a hell?
How long, O God, on the earth of Mi'raj
    will justice seem to be just a mirage?
The thirsty crowd 'round and find naught but You
    but where is Your reckoning, so swift and true?

The balance seems all torn *apart* and askew
how can they *hide* what is in such clear view?

On one side, death's collateral, on one, it's tragedy
oppression's clouds swarm all around, but gather in valleys
The sun's hiding her face in shame, moon's scarred by what he's seen
and this crop that's been sown in blood, will reap ruin's blazing sheafs

And if good for the cause, they'd try
to shoot Buraq down from the sky
The perfumed stones, pines, sparkling eyes
may not yet wither on the vine
But when will concrete cages, walls
all crumble into dust and fly?
When will the lightning answer the
thund'rous chorus of grieving sighs?

And in the face of this unyielding pain
we look to the skies and pray for Your rain
My heart will not sleep, nor my tongue relent
until You answer Quds's sad laments

Those trapped within their crimes' prison
fearing what they have done to them
Fearing the trampled fearless ones
fearing the fact that they're human
grant them all truly just freedom
next year in Jerusalem

In this year of Alif doubled Kaf[2]
we seek refuge with the people of Kahf
Before the day when You unveil Your calf
deliver us from Your fury and wrath
and all of the worshippers of golden calves

One body the believers are, and so if I forget
my siblings' cries in Palestine, may I forget my left
if we forget those living shrines
who stubbornly refuse death's lies
may my right hand forget its skill
and strength, for they are mine.

2. 2021 = ك ك ا

For Devin, Lavel, and D'Sean

The dawn will not break, the sun will not rise
Over broken hearts and red, clouded eyes

They buried them there
    And said, "enough tears"
But for this pain I
    Don't have enough tears

Their lightning smiles
    Burned to memories
By blind thunder's rage
    And shells like rough tears

The shots' echo won't
    Get out of my ears
To wash away slugs
    Who has enough tears?

We've cried 'till we've bled
    We've bled 'till we've cried
For six once-bright eyes
    Who has enough tears?

No man knows the day
    No woman, the hour
But how could three dawns
    Vanish in snuffed tears?

These grounds are soaked full
    Of black blood and fears
They're watered and choked
    With lives and tough tears

Moonless tides of grief
    Endless winds of sighs
To meet their dark rise
    Who has enough tears?

The shots outnumber
    The stars in the sky
To cry and ask why
    Who has enough tears?

Tomorrow's become
    A thrice-widowed bride
For next year I've not
    Saved up enough tears

Sympathy scattered
    Like sand on spilled lives
I saw my hope limp
    Off in handcuffs, tears

Just look at this life
    Look into these eyes
To flood this desert
    Who's cried enough tears?

My dark eyes blanched white
    from grief, like the moon
Their rivers flow, but
    It's not enough tears

In this darkling vale
    Of these savage dreams
Will this land ever
    Have drunk enough tears?

The kings of this land
    are no Solomon
Our babies, split, gone
    like wiped, cast off tears

Time's stretched my grief's tent
    Over the whole sky
But for this pain I
    Don't have enough tears

An Elegy for the Migrants

Whosoever migrates in the way of God will find upon the earth many a refuge and abundance, and whosoever forsakes his home, emigrating unto God and His Messenger, and death overtakes him, his reward will fall upon God, and God is Forgiving, Merciful

—Qur'an 4:100

Come dawn breeze and wrap your clouds
'round the bodies of the drowned
In your heavenly funeral shrouds
cradle them home safe and sound

Rolling like ink off a lawh
like all flesh returns to ground
Only skies weep for these souls
tears flow to seas without sound

Oceans were created sweet
then were bittered by our tears
As they stole our children 'cross
their vast depths year after year

Time's turned continents to sand
lives flowing out through its hand

Like twin hourglasses flipped
all falls North into their pit
Diamonds, oil, dreams all slip
while fumes rise and loosen grips
'Round these glasses' widening hips
blood and minds and hopes drip thick
All falls North into the pit
save the smoke from fires' lips
Homespun cloths all fray and rip
families dangling off of cliffs
As the earth burns, turned and tipped
over flames that laugh and lick
Life down into little sips
hungry mouths all stained and sick

People flee towards Pharaoh
    Everything is upside-down
Though he and his hosts and homes
    With their blood are drunk and drowned

Feasting, they grow thirstier
    Drinking fans their hunger's flames
Never, ever satisfied
    'till all the worlds burn the same

This is not the morning dew
    these are tears we cried for you
I have no wealth, gold, nor jewels
    just stars' burning grief for you

But the desert swallows tears
    water gone, the salt remains
Body bags have all been zipped
    leaving valleys deep with pain
Paths well-trod by shoeless feet
    mark out all the unmarked graves
Headlines echo like thunder
    dark clouds leaving without rain
Numbers hail upon the page
    always numbers without names
Names are whispered in the wind
    last breaths swirl to hurricanes
Prayers like lightning flash up-down
    cutting through the sky's dark waves
Many who crossed on were drowned
    many who drowned there were saved

Those who hurt God and His friends
    have I become one of them?
This fair castle in the clouds
    where I now have made my bed
I have seen its bloody root
    I know where this alley ends
All can see the cracks throughout
    but who would dare to repent?

Leprous and falling apart
unfeeling and without shame
Nothing human now remains
save the echo of its name

Those who leave their homes for love
always die a martyr's death
What have you to pay them back
when they come back on your breath?

What have you prepared for them?
what have you cooked up for us?
When the skies are rolled away
when the mountains fly like thrush?

When the graves are overturned
when the souls' secrets are spilt
Then each sleeping dreamer sees
upon what his house is built

When time is up for itself
and when death is sacrificed
When hunger has had its fill
when the fire melts to ice

When the eyes become iron
When the sky's frozen to stone
When sun's ashes fall like snow
When the earth's bones boil to foam

When the seas' flame trees have grown
Then we'll see what's owned, who owns
And what every soul is owed
All unknowns raised up and shown

But this when is only now
there is no time left to waste
But I still can't figure out
how we can escape this place

Who knows how words once spoken
can all return to your mouth?
I imagine it's just like
flocks of birds all flying south

If this life's the key what's the
    lock, and door, and what's behind?
And with your ocean's mercy
    why's there any need to hide?

Five things have never been seen:
    water, mirrors, light, dark, and eyes
But I saw them all within
    the cloud of your lovelorn sigh

The whole world is full of you
    but you're nowhere to be found
Like the meaning of these words
    you're the shadow, sun, and ground

So please requite all of them
    and please don't yet quit on us
Quietly you tell your friends
    without them, no hope for us

How could these scales be balanced?
    all this blood against those dreams?
All these hearts heavy with love,
    with this grief straining the seams
How can you measure what's real
    up against what only seems?
What does your justice look like
    to those who've seen what they've seen?

Come down breeze and wrap your clouds
    'round all those that love has crowned

All those who drown get across
    all who enter love's sea drown

For Our Father

Snowflakes float glistening toward the ground
    until the sunlight brings them round
and back again to heaven's clouds
    our losses here are all there found

We flounder here, they're lost in bliss
    soaring the depths or in skies drowned
'Twixt lightning strikes that never miss
    in shoreless seas of joy unbound

Lives, seasons, aeons dry like rain
    then fall back to the earth again
Our father, much more than a friend
    if you must go, let's meet again

Born in a palace in the spring
    into this world he came rushing—
Headlong—like a stone skipped across
    the waves of this world's shiny dross
Headstrong—with wisdom's intellect
    cutting through obstacles unchecked

With roots sunk deep in holy streams
    he bore fruit and more gifts unseen
Straight as iron, and sharp as steel
    bright as sunbeams, but yet more real
Than dreams that filled his blessed head
    some spoken, still more left unsaid
As soft as cloth but tough as trees
    bending, not breaking, in storms' breeze

His character's like a fire at night,
    a pillar of cloud seen in the daylight
A slight giant whose shadow dwarves mountains
    whose light brightened faces and hearts past counting

On Harmattan winds, he flew to the West
    carrying from home, all that he thought best
bringing new life to old, dried out lands
    breaking new ground with hard-working hands

And up against the rising floods
    he built a hedge of thorns and blood
tending his flock, his garden within
    fighting off sickness, diseases, and sin
cultivating life, virtue, and discipline
    unwavering as the roots of mountains
tempered with mercy, and gen'rosity
    with bountiful grace as wide as seas
    humble, sincere—just as it should be
Kindness is not weakness, nor ev'n folly
    but rather strength pushed to its apogee

He gave and he gave and he lent
    and he learned and he spent and he taught
Never taking without giving
    never giving second thoughts
Hoarding only virtues—hard won and fought—
    treasures of a life by righteousness wrought
And then as leaves began to Fall
    in sunset hues—he got the call
to come back to his Father's home
    having made good on this life's loan

And, as always, with dignity, he
    shouldered the weight, faced his duty
through pain and tears, he set aside fear
    ready and poised to fly on and free

A shooting star, a comet so bright
    Its trail can never fade from our sight
And like a distant, blue supernova
    we bask in its light, after it's over

But life without you just cannot be thought
    like sunless days, like fires not hot
Like songs without tune, like sight without place
    And yet, even so, that is what we face

But you can't be distant
  nor we ever part
With your voice in our ears
  your spirit in our hearts
With your blood in our veins
  And your thoughts on our brains
But even so, we still long, it seems
  to be with you, beyond all these dreams

Obscure day of undying light
  go gently in that brighter night
Of peace, just peace and rest in sight
  peace, only peace, after the fight
Peace, only peace, all wrongs made right
  peace, only peace abides in might
Peace, only peace, we pray tonight
  with hands clasped tight 'till morning light
As long as doves dance with dawn songs
  as long as stars pierce black with white
As long as snow falls and is drawn
  heavenward, glistening in dawn's light

A dupe lọwọ Ọlọrun Ọba
Oluwaṣeun, ẹ ṣe o Baba

Broken

Lightning breaks dark's hold, dusk breaks sky's blue cold
    my tears broke the drought, but dry, grief untold

The wind makes dunes roll, fate's waves, crashing slow
    they break and bury all under sands' gold

Regret, love, and time broke off the blindfolds
    of the loveliest story ever told

The reed's cry rises from cuts and wells' holes
    I'm the sound of my heart breaking open

Passion's outbreak made bodies break in souls
    When beauty's mirror cracked, love strolled unbroken

My past's a mirage, now beneath your soles
    the future's a heap of bones, old, broken

Muddled, mistaking stars in puddle's hold
    for heaven's depths we dived in, necks broken

To follow knowledge like a sinking stone
    we made of prison, a palace broken

Once proudly laughing at tales of sea's shoals
    we bubbles are foam, waves humbled, broken

We come to you cracked, eyes shut, wounds open
    words, bonds, and pacts, backs, promises broken

To see what your sun and moon mirrors behold
    we climb falling stars, piled-up dreams broken

And diving into your dark pupil's hole
    you fill our eyes—vision's colors broken

When you broke out into songs from back home
    angels cut their hands, wings ruffled, broken

These words are the sound of veils coming down
    your shirt lies open, seams ripped and broken

How could these secrets be spoken untold?
    ocean's silent vow, your breeze has broken

Perfection burned jealous of your eyes' kohl
    the point of your mole broke beauty's own mold

All loves are the fringes of your black stole
    lives, broken, bought, sold, from your hair, we stole

Only broken teeth get covered in gold
    only broken hearts can hold glory's coals

Only when we're broken down, we're consoled
    by union, like numbers raised by one's pole

Your love in my heart broke brokenness whole
    all souls are mended in your threshold's mold

And what you lay down is what we uphold
    we take what your two lips give and withhold

As long as lightning's flash vanishes bold
    and silence breaks in thunder's echoed rolls

As long as the new precedes all the old
    and clouds' falling tears break heaven's control

As long as the sun breaks dawn in sky's bowl
    as long as time breaks fate's seals, scrolls unfold

As long as love breaks through space and time's hold
    and I complete you, as broken mends whole

Khalwa

At the peak of my soul's depths
    I sit in silent reverie
The sun above, weather below
    The bright blue breathes in, out of me

Index of First Lines

A

B

C

D

E

F

H

I

L

M

W

Y

تقريظات

Endorsements

Ogunnaike's anthology takes readers on a deeply personal journey through words, worlds, and wisdom, and ultimately beyond them. At a time in which so many artists are preoccupied with self-expression, it is a pleasure to find one who has somehow managed to express selflessness so elegantly. Each poem is a confluence of different voices, cultures, dimensions, emotions, and epochs all flowing into one shoreless, floorless ocean of Love.... Read this book if you wish to swim in that ocean, but know that the most delightful drowning is inevitable.

Imam Adeyinka Muhammad Mendes,
author of *The Spirits of Black Folk: Sages Through the Ages*

The Book of Clouds veils the intellect, the deep reading of Sufi poetry, and the inner state of its author in words, yet precisely by veiling allows us to gaze and contemplate. Ogunnaike's verse allows the Islamic ghazal tradition to flow into English through rivulets, whirlpools and torrents of love, in image upon image, each producing the aesthetic of wonder that poets in any number of Islamic languages have sought to evoke for centuries. There is magic in these words.

Nicholas Boylston,
Assistant Professor of Persian Literature,
Harvard University

For more than a millennium, poetic hymns celebrating the endless facets of divine and human love—often set to local musical traditions—have become central to a host of Islamic languages, cultures and ritual observances, from West Africa across to Indonesia. Throughout that period, those poems of praise and longing often grew out of a common set of originally Arabic themes, imagery, and a shared set of poetic genres, meters and rhymes. In his The Book of Clouds, Oludamini Ogunnaike's remarkable, wide-ranging collection of original poems, he has creatively adapted his own contemporary insights and inspirations into deeply moving English verse drawing on all of those earlier genres. His always personally revealing poems here range from more familiar religious and devotional subjects to elegies inspired by heartbreaking current events."

James Morris,
author of *The Reflective Heart: Discovering Spiritual Intelligence in Ibn Arabi's Meccan Illuminations*

Oludamini Ogunnaike has penned an exquisite banquet of poetry that points to the inner landscape of a contemporary seeker in pursuit of Divine Nearness and immersion in love of the Beloved ﷺ. In this rich and enriching collection of poetry, Ogunnaike observes traditional Arabic poetic forms, yet the voice of this seeker is expressed in English, opening up the treasure chest of Sufi poetry for Western readers. This collection is an important testimony to the continuation of the living spirit of Sufi tradition in the contemporary era; although its roots lie in Eastern lands, the soul of Sufism is clearly flourishing in the West.

Sukina Noor,
author of *Love and Longing: Yearning for the Face of God*

According to the sages, poetry is primarily a way of perceiving and only secondarily a mode of expression. The word for poet in the Arabic language comes from the root meaning, 'to be aware.' The words of an inspired poet are the result of inner vision and thus offer a threshold to deeper awareness. As one steeped in the living tradition of Sufi poetry across time and space, Oludamini offers us, through these poems, and entry point into the eternal spring of Divine Unity that is also called love.

Baraka Blue,
author of *The Art of Remembrance*

The noblest and cruelest of worldly and celestial meanings are at times intoxicatingly diffused, and at others numinously seized and bravely resisted by Oludamini Ogunnaike's multilingual musings, multicultural wizardry, and multidimensional scoping.

Nizar Hermes,
Associate Professor, Dept. of Middle Eastern and South Asian Languages and Cultures, University of Virginia, author of *The City in Arabic Literature: Classical and Modern Perspectives*

Ogunnaike's profoundly inspired *Book of Clouds* is a work of firmly transcendent beauty in which the metaphor of the cloud stands for the hidden nature of the divine and the secrecy of supernature. The rhythms and thoroughly implicit sonority of these lines take the Reader toward a vision of how the unspeakable and unseen can be represented through fine diction and perfect picturing. These are words of great devotion and mastery in which the poet delivers his apprehension of a unique Godhead as depicted through the medium of written and at times melodic speech. Working from and within the tradition of West African and Persian Sufism, Ogunnaike advances those systems of poetics and faithful zeal with the force of his own terrific genius and experience: this poetry is truly active, it is not hypothetical. This is the just poetry of love where affection and intimacy are vehicles which commit the speaker—through his willing participation in the invisible—to the certain and moral implications of that kind of knowing. As the author says, "I have never seen my love wear clothes," for his beloved is the gracious presence of truth in the kosmos and is not simply worldly nor only sublunar. The poetry of this book is an illustrated memoir of that romance, one that is both impersonal and yet absolutely receptive of all possible sensibility and literal satisfaction. These poems of true intoxication represent a direct and immediate transmission of complete life: formed of inspiration, tradition, and experience. Their sharply passionate and finely rendered well-tempered metaphors will transport the Reader with their extraordinary vitality and beauty to a place that is both changeless and always stable. As the poet says, "I am rain and you are my cloud ... I am your sacrifice today." This book is a perfect mirror of that one most transparent and weightless universe and to hold it in one's hands is to receive a perfect gift.

Kevin McGrath,
Associate of the Department of South Asian Studies
and poet-in-residence at Lowell House,
Harvard University

About the Author

Oludamini Ogunnaike is an Associate Professor of Religious Studies at the University of Virginia and the author of *Deep Knowledge: Ways of Knowing in Tijani Sufism and Ifa* and *Poetry in Praise of Prophetic Perfection: West African Madīḥ Poetry and its Precedents*. This is his first published book of original poetry.

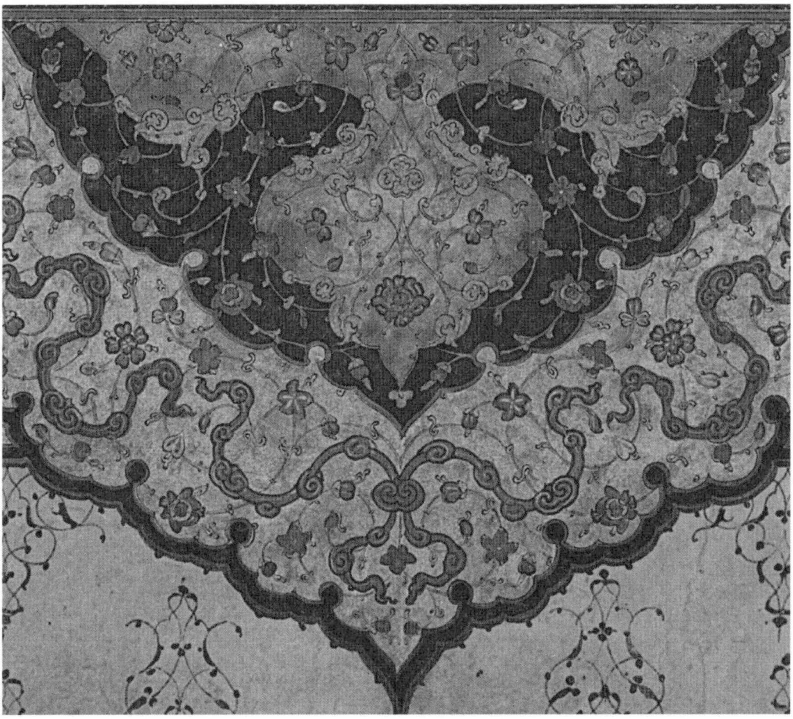